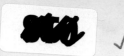

BROAD
STRIPES
AND
BRIGHT
STARS

Westminster Press Books
by
MARION MARSH BROWN

Young Nathan
The Swamp Fox
Frontier Beacon
Broad Stripes and Bright Stars

BROAD STRIPES AND BRIGHT STARS

Marion Marsh Brown

Illustrations by
LYLE JUSTIS

Philadelphia
THE WESTMINSTER PRESS

Library of Congress Catalog Card Number: 54-11628

To
all young Americans
who love their flag

CONTENTS

1. Proud Day   9
2. The Fox Hunt   16
3. Off to School   24
4. " Curly Key "   31
5. The Flag Still Flies   38
6. The Race   46
7. First Love   54
8. Back to the City   64
9. Mary Lloyd   71
10. " To Mary "   80
11. First Hurdles   87
12. Bad Luck and Good   94
13. On the Potomac   102
14. Introductions   110
15. Politics   118
16. The Star-spangled Flag   127

7

17. Treason 134

18. War 144

19. Soldiering 150

20. Red Sky 157

21. A Prisoner 166

22. With His Majesty's Fleet 174

23. " O Say, Can You See " 185

24. Fulfillment 197

1

PROUD DAY

This is the last thing we have to do," Frank said, breathing hard from the exertion and the heat. He had just unrolled a large American flag, and he held it briefly in his hands, thinking that the blue field in the corner, with its circle of bright stars, looked like a patch of night sky that had caught a cluster of stars playing "ring-around-a-rosy." Ordinarily, he would have spoken his thoughts to his sister, Ann, who stood watching him, but just now he didn't have time.

He reached above his head to place the flag over the exact center of the white-pillared portico.

" We have to get cleaned up," Ann said. " You ought to see your face."

" I can see yours," Frank said, grinning and standing back to survey his work.

There was a hot wind blowing, and though it swirled red dust about the children in eddies, it also spread the flag in lovely ripples like the waves in ripe grain.

" The flag looks beautiful, Frank! "

Frank nodded, ran his hand through his rumpled curly hair, and glanced at the sun. " Come on. We have to hurry! " he urged. " General Washington is likely to be here any minute."

" Papa left hours ago to meet him," Ann said as they started into the house.

" Before dawn," Frank agreed. " But he was going all the way to Frederick."

" Isn't Mr. Washington an ex-general now? " Ann asked.

Frank laughed. " You don't become an ex-general. You keep a military title for life, once you've earned it. But he *is* the ex-President now. — Umm! Smell that ham," he added as they reached the cool, dusky interior of the house.

" Yummy! " cried Ann. " I can hardly wait till General Washington gets here so we can eat."

Frank eyed her coldly. " Honestly, Ann! " he said. " All you think about's your stomach. Don't you realize what an honor it is to have George Washington visit Terra Rubra? "

" Of course I realize, but I'm hungry too."

" Why, we might never have had the opportunity of meeting Mr. Washington if Papa hadn't fought under him in the Revolution."

" I know. I've heard about it often enough."

" Well, you ought to be proud. You're about as patriotic as a flea."

Ann stuck out her tongue at him, and picking up her long, full skirts, ran up the winding staircase and disappeared into her room.

Frank followed more slowly. He was thinking how the flag had looked after he had it hung. There was something about the young flag of his country, with its brave red and white stripes and its rich field of blue starred with white, that thrilled him deeply. Perhaps it was the story of how Betsy Ross had designed it; perhaps the fact that his father had fought under it; or perhaps what it stood for: the United States of America. It was wonderful to be growing up in a new country with its own government and its own flag. " We, the people of the United States, in order to form a more perfect Union — " The sonorous words of the Preamble to the Constitution, which his father had set him to learn, rang in his ears.

He opened the door to his room slowly, though moments before he had been urging Ann to hurry. This new nation in whose birth his father and George Washington had assisted had not long been a nation. He himself was six when the Revolution ended and his father came home from the war. He was fourteen now. Eight years.

Suddenly he caught sight of himself in the little mirror above his washstand and laughed aloud. He looked like a zebra, his moist face streaked with red dust. No wonder Ann had chided him. Terra Rubra! Red Earth! His grandfather had named the Key estate well. The soil was as red as brick dust, and how it stuck to you, dust or mud! But then he remembered he must hurry.

He was brushing his hair vehemently in an effort to get it to lie flat when he heard a commotion outside. His father and the General! Why did I have to be born with this curly hair? he thought for the thousandth time, dropping the brush and making a dash for the stairs. Ann was ahead of him. He raced past her, but stopped,

suddenly shy, at the front door. Outside were scores of
men, most of them wearing the faded and tattered old
uniforms they had worn in his father's regiment. Some
approached on horseback; others dismounted at the hitching rack. The servants took the horses as men shouted
greetings. Where were his father and General Washington?

When he discovered them, they were almost upon him.
He had pushed open the door, and with Ann at his side
had stepped out onto the porch, when his father and a
tall, distinguished-looking gentleman with white hair
came up the steps.

" We'll go inside and clean up a bit before dinner,
General," his father was saying, when he caught sight of
Ann and Frank. He stopped, his hand on the General's
elbow.

" General Washington," he said, " may I have the
honor of presenting my children, Ann Charlton Key and
Francis Scott Key."

Ann curtsied prettily, and Frank bowed low, his heart
beating like a trip hammer.

" Miss Ann." The General bowed over her hand.

" Master Francis."

Frank felt his hand gripped hard, and a rush of exultation filled him. George Washington was a man's man, just
as he had dreamed he would be. He was just what his
father had said he was: " A great man, born to be a
leader of men." And the great man was gripping his
hand! Furthermore, he was addressing him: " Your father tells me you put up the flag to welcome me. Thank
you, Son. That was a fine thing for you to do; I appreciate

it. I hope you will always love and honor our flag."

" I — I'm sure I will, Sir," Frank stammered.

His father and the General moved on into the house, and Frank could see his mother coming to meet them. Then the door closed and he stood staring at it as if dazed.

" Well," Ann said, " you can't see through a closed door. Let's see what's going on out here."

Frank followed her across the porch and into the yard where the men were milling about, but they didn't interest him. Many he recognized as neighbors or old acquaintances of his father's who had stopped before at Terra Rubra to enjoy the good food at the Key table. The servants had set up benches with rows of washbasins on them, and the men were throwing water over their dusty faces and wiping the red dirt onto the clean white towels that had been provided for them. These men were just common mortals. Inside was General Washington!

" Let's go in," he said to Ann.

" All right. We'll surely get to eat soon."

Frank could scarcely believe his good luck. He had thought he would have to eat with Ann and his mother, or at best with the old soldiers on the lawn, but his father was motioning him to come to Mr. Washington's table.

Of course he didn't get to sit close to the General. There were important gentlemen present whose Army rank or official position in the village of Frederick gave them that privilege. But at least he was at the same table with him, and, if he listened very closely, he could catch his words now and then.

Finally chairs scraped back from the table, and Frank edged closer to his father and his guest. " Well, General," his father was saying, " you promised to give us a few words. I believe if you would speak from the upstairs portico, everybody could see and hear you. Frank, will you be kind enough to take the General up? I'll follow shortly."

" Certainly. This way, Sir." Frank led the way up the stairs and down the hall to the French doors that opened onto the long upstairs porch which ran the length of the house. He saw at once that the crowd had swelled tremendously. Countless women and children had joined the men. Every carriage in Frederick County must have disgorged itself of a brimming load!

" Law, General Washington," Frank said with a gulp. " I never saw so many people. You'd better say something good." Then he realized what he had said and blushed scarlet.

But General Washington put a hand on his shoulder and laughed heartily. " I'll try, Son. That's all any of us can do." Then he turned serious. " You know what I'm going to do? " he said. " I'm going to stand right by your flag. Then I'm sure I can say something good."

Frank smiled self-consciously. " Here comes Father," he said. " I'll run on down if you don't mind."

" Of course, Son, run along."

He could scarcely push through the crowd as he reached the front lawn, but he was slight and quick as an eel so he soon had the position he wanted, directly below the General. He turned his face up and waited breathlessly. The crowd grew still.

" My countrymen," the General's voice came down to them, ringing and clear, " I am about to leave your good land, your beautiful valleys, your refreshing streams, and the blue hills of Maryland which stretch before me. I cannot leave you, fellow citizens, without thanking you again and again for the true and devoted friendship you have shown me. In the darkest hours of the Revolution, of doubt and gloom, the succor and support I received from the people of Frederick County always cheered me. It always woke a responsive echo in my heart. My heart is too full to say more. God bless you all."

For an instant there was silence. Then thunderous applause broke out. Men shouted and threw their old cockaded caps into the air. " Hurrah! Hurrah for General Washington! "

Frank shouted with them until his throat was hoarse with the shouting and the dust. Then he realized that his father and General Washington were preparing to mount. His father was going to ride as far as Taneytown with the General. Frank pressed through the crowd. The General saw him coming and extended his hand. " I am glad to have met you, Son. I'm sure you'll be a man to make your father proud. Remember what I said about the flag."

" I won't forget, General Washington — not ever."

on the newel and gave his nephew his full attention.

" Because you were born in America," Frank said,
" and because your family was here, and because you intended to make this your home."

" Spoken like a lawyer, Frank," Uncle Philip said.
" Perhaps you'll study law and come in with me one day.
You know I'm going into the practice in Annapolis."

" Yes, Papa told me."

" Someday when we have a little time I'll give you my
reasons on the other side of the case you just summed up
so nicely. Yet perhaps the whole thing's best forgotten."

They moved on into the dining room, and Frank lost
his uncle in the maze of red coats. His throat began to
tighten and his stomach to jump. He wondered how these
men could eat great plates of ham and eggs and fried
potatoes and gulp mugs of steaming coffee.

Suddenly the sharp, shrill, winding notes of the horn
gave warning that the hunt master was ready. As the men
swallowed the last of their food, Frank made a quick dash
from the room. The food laid no hold on him. This was
the moment he had been waiting for. The moment he
had been living for! Who would be his riding partner?
He hoped it would be someone he knew.

He saw Mose holding his horse. Comet's russet coat
shone, and the old colored man's face was wreathed in
smiles. " Good luck, Massa Frank," he said as Frank put
his foot in the stirrup.

" Thanks, Mose." Comet was impatient to be off. He's
as nervous as I am, Frank thought. " Good boy," he said
soothingly and patted the quivering neck.

As he turned his horse, he saw that his uncle was beside him.

" We're riding together," Uncle Philip said.

" Good! " It didn't half express what he felt. He flashed a smile at his uncle.

" I think it's good," Uncle Philip said. " If the hounds don't find the fox's lair too soon, you and I should have a good visit."

The notes of the horn cut in, the hounds were released, and Frank's heart became a pounding dynamo. They were off!

But the hounds were slow in finding the scent, and Frank was very glad to have his uncle at his side.

" I suppose you've heard the story of how your father divided his inheritance equally with me," his uncle said as they rode along.

Frank nodded. " I think it's funny Grandfather left it all to him in the first place," he said.

" That was the Old Country way," Philip explained. " Everything to the eldest son."

" I'll bet people won't do that any more, now that we're a democracy."

" They'll gradually get away from it, no doubt," his uncle agreed. " I suppose you know too that your United States Government confiscated all the land your father had given me, because I was fighting with the British? "

Frank nodded again. " Only it wasn't the United States Government then," he said. " It was the Colonial Government."

" My lawyer friend again! " Uncle Philip laughed.

" But do you know what your father is proposing now? "
Frank shook his head.

" Last night he told me," Uncle Philip said, his voice
serious, " that he was going to divide with me again;
give me half of the lands he has left. I told him I didn't
think that would be fair to you. I made him promise not
to do anything until we'd had a chance to talk to you.
After all, he would be giving away half of your future inheritance."

" I think that's splendid, Uncle Philip! "

" Splendid? To lose half your inheritance at a snap of
your fingers? "

Frank smiled. " I'm sure there'll be plenty left for me.
Anyhow, I expect to make my own way in the world."

" I'm sure you will, and that you'll do a good job of it."

" I'm very proud of Papa."

" You should be. He's one of the most tolerant and
generous men alive."

" And I'm glad you're to have the inheritance, Uncle
Philip. It will help you get a start. Your being exiled to
England after the war kept you from getting established."

" But always remember, Frank, I wouldn't have been
exiled if I'd fought with the Colonists, nor would I
have lost half of your father's lands. But I do want you
to know this: I was doing what I thought was right."

" I'm sure of it, Uncle Philip."

They were entering a woods on a neighboring estate.
The hounds were having trouble this morning. Frank
and his uncle had lagged to the rear of the hunt, but
now Uncle Philip spurred his horse. " Listen! " he said.
There was excitement in his voice.

The sound of the horn wound back to them.

Instantly Frank touched his spurs lightly to Comet's sides, and they were off, leaping fallen logs, fording a glistening stream, racing toward the spot where the other hunters were gathered. Frank's heart was high with adventure.

The hounds had found a fox's earth at last. They would soon have the fellow out, and dogs and men alike would be after him. The thrill of anticipation made Frank's scalp tingle. This time he did not have to turn back. This time he would be a part of the mad chase across fields and fences. He felt every bit a man, with his uncle's conversation still ringing in his ears and the mad barking of the hounds calling him.

Suddenly the notes of the hunt master's horn shrilled again. Though he had raised himself in the stirrups, Frank had not been able to see past the men to where the hounds were digging. But now he saw something that made his heart stand still. A red streak flashed over a lit-

tle hillock not thirty feet from him. He spurred his horse
and was at the head of the chase. The hounds crowded in,
other horsemen flanked him and pushed ahead, but he
kept his place close in the front ranks. He lay low against
his horse. " Faster, boy! Good Comet! Faster! Faster! "
The horse lengthened out as they flew across a level
meadow. A fence loomed up. Frank crouched for the
jump. " Good boy! " It was a beautiful jump. How often
he and Comet had practiced this together! But this was
not practice; this was real.

They were in a woods again. Slower now, watching the
trees. The dogs were outdistancing the horses. But their
mad yelping and the horn's shrill cry pulled the men
like a mighty magnet.

The sun was climbing high, and the horses' sides began to heave. Suddenly the note of the horn took on a
different cry. It sounded exultant; yet at the same time
it seemed to sound a warning and a command.

Frank knew instinctively what it meant. He began rein-
ing his horse. Even so, he almost passed them — the hunt
master, the hounds, his father. He himself was the third
man to draw rein. But what he saw did not fill him with
the exultation that the chase had. It made him a trifle
sick.

The hounds had made the kill, and the hunt master's
servant was handing the fox to his master. The hunt
master held it up by its beautiful bushy red tail for all to
see. Its throat was dripping blood. The body that minutes before had been so vigorously alive hung limp.
Frank couldn't help feeling sorry. He turned aside, trying to locate his uncle, but he couldn't see him. Suddenly

his father's voice was beside him. " Good riding, Son. It isn't often that a man on his first hunt is in on the death."

Then Frank heard the hunt master's voice speaking his name. " Master Francis Key! A new man on the hunt, and among the first at the kill. The brush goes to Master Francis Key! "

Frank turned in his saddle and saw that the hunt master's servant was bringing him the fox's tail. He shuddered. He didn't want it. Then he heard his father's voice at his side again, quiet but firm: " It's an honor, Son." Automatically he reached out to take the brush.

Everyone crowded around him.

" The brush to Squire Key's son! "

" And the lad's first hunt."

Finally Uncle Philip said, " I think we may start home now, Nephew."

Frank was glad. He was suddenly very hot and very tired. With the beautiful red tail waving like a plume from the pommel of his saddle, he turned his horse's head homeward.

3

OFF TO SCHOOL

I wish *I* was going," Ann sighed. She and Frank were sitting beside the brook that ran through the Terra Rubra woods, watching the glint of silver where the sun struck slantwise through the trees to touch the water.

" Not really, you don't," Frank said. " Not to stay, like I have to."

" Oh, but to see all the new gowns in the shops, and the fashionable ladies in their fine carriages on the streets — and Uncle Philip! "

" Yes, Uncle Philip's a bright spot. I wish I was going to stay with him. I think he wanted me to, but I guess Papa was afraid I'd be exposed to too gay a life."

" I can just imagine the parties at Uncle Philip's, can't you? " Ann clasped her hands around her knees ecstatically. " With Uncle Philip the gayest one of all, surrounded by pretty ladies laughing at his jokes and fluttering their fans."

Frank nodded. " I can also imagine how it will be at Great-aunt Scott's," he said. " As gay as a bottle of doom."

Ann laughed. " But you'll make friends at school," she

said, " and you really do want to be educated, don't you? "

Frank smiled wryly and poked at a patch of moss with a stick. " I suppose," he agreed. " But what I'd like best would be to go on living here at Terra Rubra with you and Mamma and Papa." His voice was dreamy.

" We have such fun, don't we? "

Frank nodded. " That's why it's hard for me to leave. But I guess we have to grow up someday. I have to think about a career; and before long some handsome young man will come along and carry you off."

" Silly! " Ann scoffed.

" But true." Frank unscrambled his long legs and stood up. " Come on and help me decide what to lay out for Mose to pack," he said. " It's Wednesday already, and Friday will be here before I have time to spit."

By Thursday, the whole household was in a stir, getting Frank ready to leave on horseback for Annapolis the following morning. Mose and his father would ride with him the eighty miles.

It wouldn't be the first time Frank had been to the city. He and Ann had often visited their blind little Grandmother Key at Belvoir, and their mother had taken them on into Annapolis to visit the other relatives and see the sights. It had always been exciting. But on the other occasions he had gone by carriage, and there was always the anticipation of the return to Terra Rubra at the end of the stay. This time he must remain in Annapolis the entire winter — without Ann. He was homesick before he started.

He escaped the confusion in the house and slipped out

to the fragrant hayloft. He lay on his back and let his
body sink into the loosely piled new hay. How could he
bear to leave all this? And yet, as he had told his Uncle
Philip, he did want to do something with his life, and
that meant he must get an education. A vision of the flag
flying for General Washington's visit drifted before his
eyes. I want to do something worthy of it, he thought,
something that will bring honor to it. I don't mean fighting in a war. Of course I'd do that if I had to, but there
must be other things.

Then his mind drifted back to Terra Rubra and the
life that he must leave.

> " Terra Rubra," he said aloud, " land of red earth,
> You have bound me to you from the day of my birth."

He reached into his pocket and drew out a stub of a
pencil and a scrap of paper. One of the things he and Ann
loved to do was to compose poems. He would write her
one for a going-away present. He put down the words
he had just spoken aloud, chewed the pencil stub a moment, then added two more lines:

> " Your woods and your fields, your meadows and hills,
> Blue sky overhead, reflected in rills."

The next two came easily:

> " The joy and the peace and the bliss I have known,
> As over me gently the west winds have blown — "

The sound of Mose persistently calling his name interrupted his thoughts. " Massa Frank! Massa Frank! "

Reluctantly he crawled out of his nest in the hay, brushed himself off, and started down the ladder. He would have to leave the poem till night.

Long before daylight the next morning, Mose came in to light his fire. The fated day was here. Frank crawled out of bed to copy his poem for Ann. He'd thought of the other two lines, but he'd had no opportunity to write them down. He dipped his quill pen into the ink and wrote rapidly, for they would soon be calling him to breakfast. The first two couplets were better than the last, but Ann would understand.

" The joy and the peace and the bliss I have known," he copied.

Then he added the final lines:

> " Are like nothing, no nothing I ever shall find,
>   Whatever I do and where'er my paths wind."

There was a knock at his door. " Massa Frank, Ise come to get your things. Breakfus' am ready."

" I'll be right down, Mose."

He gave one last, lingering look around his room, then ran downstairs. Now that the time to leave had come, he was buoyed up by excitement. A journey was always exciting, and starting out with his father and Mose on horseback gave this one added zest. And even though he hated to leave Terra Rubra, entering school at St. John's, meeting other boys and making friends with them held the thrill of the new and untried. It would be his first experi-

ence with school and almost his first association with
other boys. He had received his education thus far from
his mother and father. Ann had been his only school-
mate; his father's study, his only schoolroom.

Breakfast was over. Frank had felt the same lack of interest in food that he had on hunt morning.

"Ise got all Massa Frank's luggage strapped to the
pack horse," Mose said at the door.

" Well, we'd as well get started," Mr. Key said.

Frank turned to his mother. " Good-by, Mamma. See
you next spring."

His mother stood very straight. " Take good care of
yourself, Frankie. We'll miss you." There were tears in
her eyes, but she smiled. He kissed her cheek, then turned
to look for Ann. She had disappeared. He hoped she
wasn't off somewhere crying.

He followed his father to the hitching rack, where the
horses stood waiting, stomping impatiently. It was still
dark, and the air was chill with autumn frost.

He heard his mother's voice from the porch. " Put
your coat on, Ann," she said. " It's cold."

So Ann was coming out! He was glad. He stood waiting to mount, watching the dim figures of his mother and
sister approach through the gloom.

When Ann reached his side, he slipped a paper into
her coat pocket. " Here's a poem," he said.

" And here's a present I made for you." She held out a
package.

" A present? Thanks, Ann. Thanks ever so much. I
guess I have to go now. Take care of Terra Rubra."

" I'll try. Good-by, Frank." Her voice was unsteady.

" Good-by, Ann."

He put his foot in the stirrup. " Can't I know what's in the package? " he asked, placing it on the saddle in front of him.

" When it gets light enough to see, you can open it if you want to."

" Fine! I'll want to. And I know I'll like it."

" Good-by! " Mr. Key called. " I'll be back next week." He turned his horse toward the lane.

Frank followed, tingling from excitement and the frost in the air. This was adventure! He was going into a new world, a new life. What would it hold for him?

By eight o'clock they had reached Taneytown.

" We'll stop and rest the horses a bit," Mr. Key said. " I have some business to attend to. Frank, do you want to come with me, or do you want to go with Mose to water the horses? "

" I'll go with Mose," Frank said. He had been thinking for some time of opening Ann's present. This was his opportunity.

Mose was heading down Main Street toward the village watering trough, and Frank followed. When he had dismounted and Mose had taken his horse, he sat on a crude wooden bench that he knew from experience would soon be occupied by the village loafers. But this early in the morning, he had it to himself. He fumbled at the parcel. Something she'd made, Ann had said. He missed her already. He was very glad to have her present. He laid back the paper and saw a soft heap of red and white. His heartbeat quickened. With both hands he lifted the folded cloth and let it fall free. An American flag!

" It's beautiful, Ann," he murmured. He held it out at arm's length, and the morning sun struck it full. " What broad stripes and bright stars! " he exclaimed. " Look, Mose," he called. " Look what Miss Ann made me. Isn't it beautiful? "

" Sho' am, Massa Frank. Sho' am pow'ful purty."

It's the very nicest thing she could have done, Frank thought. I'll keep it always. And I'll try to do something for my country that is worthy of it.

Gently he refolded the flag; but instead of putting it back in its wrappings, he buttoned it carefully under his jacket. He would take no chances of anything's happening to it on the journey.

4

"CURLY KEY"

Frank and his father had stopped the second night at Grandmother Key's, and now were on the last lap of their journey.

" We should be there by noon," Mr. Key said as they jogged along through the bright autumn morning. The sky was a deep, bright blue, and the sun made diamond lace of the frosted weed stalks at the side of the road.

" Will we go right to St. John's? " Frank asked.

" I think so. I'd like to get you enrolled, and then with our business taken care of, we can have the evening to visit Philip." His father's voice took on warmth as he spoke of his brother, and Frank understood. He felt that way about Uncle Philip too.

There were so many things to think about that the miles didn't seem long. There was the past evening at Grandmother's; the afternoon and evening ahead; the days to follow, when his father would have returned to Terra Rubra and he would be a student at St. John's.

Last night he had taken his flag in to " show " his grandmother. Her veined hands had caressed it lovingly. " Think of all it stands for, Frankie," she said in her soft voice: " Our country that your father fought to make free; all the brave men and women in it; the responsibility of a free people; the future of all the young folks like you and Ann — " He watched her face as she spoke and marveled at its repose. Grandmother had been blind since she was a young girl. The story of how she had lost her sight never ceased to thrill him. Time and again he had heard it: how the slave quarters on her father's estate had caught fire in the night, and Grandmother, then a beautiful young girl, had dashed into the flaming cabins and carried babies from their beds and helped the old and infirm to safety. In so doing, she had lost her own sight. Frank often wondered if he or Ann could ever do a thing half so brave.

But now the sights along the road captured his attention. Carriages and tobacco carts began to appear. Annapolis couldn't be far away! What would it be like at the school? Would the other boys like him? Would they accept him?

His first impression of St. John's Preparatory School and College was of a big, ugly building set in a bare, unattractive yard. I'm going to hate it, he thought, thinking longingly of Terra Rubra with its mellowed brick and gracious lines, framed by sloping emerald lawn and bright flower beds. Then he saw an American flag flying over the building, and he felt better.

He went inside with his father. They met the headmaster, and his father paid him money, and they went out again. They didn't see any boys. " Classes will start at seven o'clock Monday morning," the headmaster said. " You will be in the First Form, Master Key."

" Yes, Sir," Frank said, feeling nothing but a cold dread. If only he could be on the road home to Terra Rubra with his father and Mose on Monday.

But as they went back out to their horses, the flag caught his eye again. " The responsibility of a free people," Grandmother Key had said. " The future of the young folks like you and Ann." If he were to be prepared to take his responsibility tomorrow, he must get an education today. He squared his shoulders.

He needed them squared, in the days to come.

" Curly! Curly! Curly, curly Key! " The taunts of the First Form boys rang in his ears all the way home to Great-aunt Scott's each night after school. It had started on Monday. In the schoolroom the boys had grinned and nudged each other and pointed at his hair. Frank had tried to ignore them, but he could feel his ears growing pink. At dismissal they had begun the open attack, and it had not lessened as the week went by, although he had tried his best to be friendly. If they would just give him a chance, they would discover he was no more of a sissy than any of them. What difference did a fellow's hair make? But it was making a lot of difference to him.

There was no one at home when he reached his great-aunt's after school on Friday. The emptiness of the big house was too much for him in his misery. He would go pay Uncle Philip a visit. He hadn't been to his office, though Uncle Philip had invited him to come. He would go now.

He started for town at a brisk pace and soon found the frame building his uncle had described, with a dry-goods store below and narrow, enclosed wooden steps at the side leading steeply upward to the offices on the second floor. He clattered up the stairs and found a door with large gold letters: " Philip Key, Esquire, Attorney at Law." Should he knock or open the door? He fumbled at the knob.

" Come in! " his uncle's voice called. " Why, Frank! What an unexpected pleasure! Come in. Come in."

Uncle Philip took his hand, and he at once felt like himself again.

" Sit down. How are things going at St. John's? "

Frank's eyes fell. " They think I'm a sissy because of my hair," he said.

Uncle Philip nodded. " Boys can be cruel, Frank. You mustn't let it bother you." He looked speculatively at his nephew. " Why don't we have your hair cut short? " he asked. " Of course, a few years from now the girls will be swooning over you, with your curly hair and big blue eyes, but I can see how they're a cross to you at present."

Frank laughed. It was just like Uncle Philip to think of something like girls swooning over him. But the real reason for his laughter was the release of tension that his uncle's suggestion afforded. " I'd sure like to get it cut, Uncle Philip. Who's your barber? "

" I'll take you to him. I was just ready to leave."

When Frank was back in his room at Great-aunt Scott's, he stood before the glass in glee. He preened. He chuckled. " Just wait till the boys see me," he said aloud.

But when Great-aunt Scott saw him at dinner, she threw up her hands in holy horror. " Oh, no! Not your beautiful hair! That wretch of a Philip. He's ruined you."

Frank didn't care what she said. All he cared about was the boys at school.

With his books under his arm, he started out briskly on Monday morning. He was early, and as he approached the school grounds, he saw that only a couple of the boys in his Form were ahead of him. The older boys didn't stand around outside the school but went directly to their rooms. Only the younger ones, in the First Form, delayed going in until the last possible moment. Frank had hoped to find all the First Formers assembled in the yard, but in his eagerness he had walked too fast.

As he approached the two boys who stood on the sidewalk, they roared with laughter. " Poor Curly," cried one, " he's been shorn! "

Frank walked to the steps and laid his books down care-

fully. Then he turned back toward the boys. He'd had
enough. He wasn't going to put up with this any longer.
He looked them over appraisingly and decided to attack
the larger one first.

The first blow was totally unexpected. It knocked the
big boy flat. Frank's confidence grew. There was time to
get in a couple of good licks on the smaller boy before
the first was up again. " I've taken all I'm going to take
off you, see? " he cried angrily, striking out with all his
strength. He reserved his best blows for the big boy and
managed to hold the smaller one off by rapid side-step-
ping and an occasional blow in his direction. His father
had taught him how to defend himself, and he was as
strong as he was agile. He'd given these boys every chance
to be decent. Now he was going to show them a thing
or two.

Suddenly he found himself sprawling flat, his mouth
full of dirt. " You tripped me, you dirty little so-and-so! "
This time he sent the smaller boy reeling. But the big
one took advantage of his instant's respite and came in
with a driving blow to Frank's stomach. Frank doubled
up, gasped a second for breath, then flew into the other
like a fury. Just one good one on the chin, he told himself grimly. Just one good one, and I'd have you.

But at that instant a bony fist landed in his nose, and
he spit blood. He was almost winded too. He ducked to
avoid another blow at his face, and came up with his
right fist aimed squarely at his opponent's jaw. Putting
every bit of strength he had into the blow, he swung.

He stepped back dizzily, batted his eyes to clear his
vision, and realized that a great cheer had gone up. He

looked about him, dazed. He was surrounded by a ring of boys. Why, all the boys in his Form must be here! And they were cheering *him*. " 'Ray, Key! 'Ray, Key! " they were shouting.

The big boy was just picking himself up uncertainly when the headmaster pushed through the crowd. The smaller one had disappeared.

" What's going on here? Don't you know fighting is forbidden in the college yard? You're a disgrace to St. John's! Look at you, Master Key. Aren't you ashamed of yourself? Master Aldrich! Get into my office this instant, both of you. You will be punished for this."

Frank didn't care at all if he were punished. He felt wonderful, even though he could feel his nose beginning to swell. In his ears rang the shouts of his classmates: " 'Ray, Key! 'Ray, Key! " It was the sweetest sound he'd heard since he left Terra Rubra.

5

THE FLAG STILL FLIES

Frank was troubled. It was the first time he had been troubled about anything at school since the second week when, once and for all, he had established his place in the First Form. Now a hint of spring was in the air, and he and his friends would not be First Formers much longer. In this fact lay the seed of his worry. Not that he minded getting through First Form! That was splendid; it would mean an end to being the much-abused bottom layer of the educational and social strata at St. John's.

But in the process of emerging from the egg as full-fledged chicks, there was this business called " First Form Day " to be gone through. In the morning, the First Formers gave Latin orations. In the afternoon, they listened to the headmaster expound on the responsibilities of being Second Formers. And in the evening — Well, the evening performance was not scheduled on the school calendar, but to the First Formers it *was* First Form Day. Each year's class tried to outdo the preceding one in some daring stunt. This year someone already had an idea. It had been whispered to Frank only this morning.

" What do you think of it, Key? " Dan Murray asked as the two boys started home from school, their arms laden with books.

Frank shook his head. " I believe we can think of something better."

" Oh? I thought it was a colossal idea. You mean you think you have a better one? "

" No-o-o," Frank said slowly. " I just think maybe somebody will come up with something more exciting."

What he really meant was that he hoped he could think of something so good that he could dissuade the boys from their present plan. For it was this plan that troubled him.

" Since we're the first class to have a class flag, it struck me as superb."

Frank nodded. He wasn't ready to voice his objections, not until he'd had time to think of an alternative suggestion that would be sure-fire. But his objections were strong and very real. He had no objection to flying the class flag. What he objected to was the plan to take the American flag down and replace it with the other. That seemed like sacrilege, and he meant to do all in his power to see that it wasn't done.

But the week went by, and he could think of nothing. Why wouldn't some scheme come to him? What was the matter with him? He *had* to think of something! Hadn't he promised General Washington he would always honor the flag? Letting it be torn from its mast wouldn't be honoring it; it would be desecrating it. He looked lovingly at the flag Ann had made for him when he left home, pinned on the wall of his bedroom at Great-aunt Scott's.

It had added brightness to his first gloomy days. It had inspired him when his spirits lagged and he was tempted to slight his studies. It was his beacon.

The next night the First Form boys were to have a meeting to lay their plans. If he couldn't think of something by then, he would simply have to try to dissuade them from taking down the flag. But could he succeed?

He went to bed in a quandary and lay awake for a long time flogging his brain for an idea. Still none came. At last he dozed. About midnight he woke with a start. He sat up in bed. He was tingling with excitement. He had a plan, full-formed! It was a good one too. He jumped out of bed and paced the cold floor in his bare feet. Why, it was perfect! It was something that had not been done before; it was daring enough to satisfy the boldest. It was ideal if only he were clever enough to put it over.

He didn't mention his plan to anyone the next day. He would save it until the evening meeting in the Murrays' carriage house.

He swung lightly along on his way to the meeting, enjoying the early spring dusk, filling his lungs with the fresh fragrance of budding trees and rain-washed earth. A light shower in the afternoon had touched the world with magic, tinting it a soft green. Of a sudden, spring had arrived, and Frank felt a great longing for Terra Rubra. What would it be like to be there now? It seemed another world. The daily schedule at school with the boys, the evenings of study in his room at Great-aunt Scott's; these had become his life. To slip back into the easygoing pastoral existence at Terra Rubra would be like stepping out of reality into fairyland. It was a fairyland that beckoned with outstretched arms.

He pulled himself up sharply. He should have his mind on what he was going to do when he reached the carriage house, instead of on Terra Rubra.

" The meeting will come to order! "

The boys seated about the carriage house loft on kegs and boxes quieted.

" You know what we're here for," Dan said, standing before the group. " First Form Day's only a couple of weeks off, and it's time we're getting our plans laid. I think everybody's heard the idea, to take the flag down off the flagpole and put our class flag up in its place, so that when Prexy and all the Upper Form boys get to school in the morning, our flag will be waving to greet them."

He paused, and a rash of talk broke out. It was pleased, anticipatory talk. Frank feared the climate was not going to be favorable for him. He looked questioningly at Dan.

Dan pounded for order. " Of course, if anybody has a better idea — " he said tentatively.

Frank looked quickly about the room. There was a general negative shaking of heads and a few loud, " No's! "

He sprang to his feet. " Mr. Chairman," he said, " I have a suggestion."

There were a couple of protests, but most of the boys seemed ready to listen.

Frank had prepared what he was going to say with care. He wanted desperately to succeed. He didn't speak long, but he spoke persuasively.

When he sat down, the cheerleader jumped up with his arms raised for a cheer. " Ray for Key! Three cheers for Key and the steer! "

The others joined in boisterously on the " Rah! Rah! Rah! "

Frank was surrounded.

" Where'd you get such a spectacular idea? "

" It will out-Caesar Caesar! "

Frank went home from the meeting well content.

There were plans to be perfected, and the annoying interruption of examinations, but before they knew it, First Form Day was upon them. The morning was bad enough, listening to all the Latin orations, but the afternoon was worse. It dragged endlessly.

At long last it was over, and the boys were free to leave the school. They planned to be back as soon as it was dark, but Frank and Dan and John had business to attend to before they returned.

When the three finally reapproached the school, it had been dark for some time, and they knew they had kept the others waiting.

" That's all right," Frank said. " They'll be all the more keen for their ride."

" We got here as soon as we could," Dan said. " I never knew a ' critter ' without brains could be so stubborn."

" Maybe he has more brains than you think," John said wryly.

The other boys had sighted them and rushed to meet them.

" You've been long enough getting here! " they cried.

" You should try dragging this animal two miles! " Dan groaned.

" Didn't he want to come play with us? "

" Is he a good wild one? "

" He'll throw you high enough," Frank said.

" Who gets the first ride? "

" Who wants it? "

They led the steer to the center of the schoolyard. He was even more difficult to manage now, excited by the noisy boys surrounding him.

" I thought we agreed to be quiet," Dan said. " If we don't watch out, we'll have Prexy up here with his lantern."

" Sh-h-h! "

" How'll we get on the brute? "

" Take a flying leap," Frank suggested.

" The one that stays on longest gets a reward," Dan promised. " He can be last in line when we're called into Prexy's office tomorrow."

" That's a bargain."

" Let's go. Who's going to be first? "

A little fellow named Al volunteered. Dan gave him a boost onto the steer's back, and Frank let loose of the rope.

" Hooray! "

" He's off! "

" He's *off* all right," Frank laughed. " He stayed on for just one leap."

One by one the boys took their turns, but no one could be said to be getting a ride. All they were getting was a lusty pitch onto the ground. But it was hilarious fun for those who watched.

" Who hasn't had a turn? " Dan asked. " Why, Key, *you* haven't! "

" That's all right. I'll get mine. John hasn't had a try."

But John's ride was like the others. It was soon over.

" All right, Key. It's you for the beast! "

Frank handed the rope to Dan and took a few steps backward.

The animal had been growing more and more excited. He was frantic now, jerking his head and angrily pawing the earth as Dan attempted to hold him.

" Don't let him get away," Dan cautioned Frank. " Remember we want to tie him by the steps to greet Prexy in the morning."

" I'll be careful," Frank said. He took three running steps and vaulted neatly onto the steer's lunging back.

The boys fell back, as head down, the animal charged madly about the yard. Frank clung to his neck for dear life. He was enjoying his wild ride as the steer bucked and pawed. He had the advantage over these city boys, and he was enjoying his advantage to the utmost.

Then suddenly he found himself hurtling through space. It didn't frighten him. He'd taken many a spill at Terra Rubra, trying to ride everything on the place that had four legs. And he knew the yard was soft from recent rains. But suddenly a sharp, violent pain shot through his head, and he realized that he had hit something other than the muddy yard. His head had struck the iron railing at the side of the steps.

For a moment he lay stunned. Then he heard the excited voices of his classmates as they crowded anxiously around.

" Are you all right? " Dan asked, bending over him.

"Except for my head," Frank said weakly, trying to joke, "and it's not worth much anyhow." He tried to sit up, and it felt as if cannon balls were exploding in his

brain. He held his head in his hands and rocked with pain. "Did somebody get the steer?" he asked after a moment.

"Sure! And we're going to tie him right here to the railing that got you."

"You're the prize winner, Key," Dan said, helping him to his feet. "You get the place at the end of the line tomorrow when we go see Prexy."

Frank swayed dizzily. "If I'm in the land of the living," he said with a groan. But he was happy. What was a little thing like an aching head as long as he knew the American flag would be flying from the flagpole as usual in the morning?

6

THE RACE

Once Frank was back at Terra Rubra, it was as if he had never been away. What a strange quirk it was in human nature that made it possible to slip back into the pattern of existence from which one had seemed totally removed!

He talked to Ann of the other life, at St. John's, but it was as if he were telling stories that had happened to someone else.

"I met Mr. Samuel Chase, the Signer of the Declaration," he told Ann one day as they sat on their favorite grassy knoll overlooking Pipe Creek.

"Did you, Frank? How exciting! Where did you meet him? What's he like?"

"I met him at Uncle Philip's. He's fat and red-faced. John Shaw and I wrote a poem about him." Frank snickered. "I guess it wasn't very nice. We called him 'Old Bacon Face.' Uncle Philip found the poem and thought it was frightfully funny. He laughed like anything."

"Can you recite it?"

"No, I don't remember it well enough." Frank had a feeling that such things were not for Ann.

" You look so different with your hair cut short and brushed flat," she said wistfully.

" You don't think it's becoming, do you? " Frank said. " But it's much pleasanter." Then he told her of his first week at school. He could laugh about it now.

But the pastoral interlude that was summer soon came to an end. Frank left Terra Rubra with a very different feeling this time. He was not beset with qualms of uncertainty. He knew what he was going into, and he knew that his place in this other world of boys and lessons was secure. He had taken his place as a leader in his Form. Second Form would have distinct advantages over First. Pleasant anticipation accompanied him on his return to St. John's.

" So the Tenth Legion is back," the Latin Master said, giving the boys of the Second Form a welcoming smile. He had affectionately dubbed them " the Tenth Legion " the year before, as they struggled through Caesar's *Gallic War*. He looked from one to another, remembering. " Still opposed to wars, Master Key? " he asked when his eyes reached Frank.

" Yes, if I have to translate volumes about them," Frank answered promptly.

The Second Form boys laughed loudly, and the Master laughed with them.

But the Master was remembering a discussion he'd had with young Key the year before, and he was not to be diverted. " But if a war should break out between our country and another power, what then? Wouldn't you fight for your flag? "

Frank had a vision of the flag flying over Terra Rubra.

and of the greatest man he had ever met standing beside
it on the upstairs balcony. " Of course I'd fight for it,"
he said huskily. " But I still think there might be more
important things you could do for your flag than fight."

The Latin Master tipped back in his chair. He was
enjoying himself. He liked to explore boys' minds. " You
mean politics? " he asked.

Frank thought a minute. " If you were a great enough
man and could be a real leader like General Washington,
then I think it would be fine to have a place in government."

" Did you ever stop to think, Master Key, that the urge
to fight in a war, and the urge to get a political office, and
the urge to win a foot race all spring from the same competitive instinct? "

No, Frank hadn't thought about that. But he had
thought about going out for the running meets this year.
He had even practiced at Terra Rubra during the summer, stretching his long legs to an even, rhythmical stride,
running the half mile up the lane, building up his wind.

He talked to Dan about the meets as they idled home
from school one afternoon. " I don't know whether I'm
good enough or not," he said, " but if I could win anything for the Second Formers, I'd like to."

" Why don't you practice every night after school? "
Dan said. " I'll be your trainer. We can go out Dover's
Road."

All through the bright fall days, Frank worked out,
Dan helping him. As time went on, Dan grew increas-
ingly excited. " I think by spring you'll be able to beat
anything on two legs — at least anything at St. John's!

Think of the prestige it will give the Second Form if you can win the mile for us."

Frank didn't know. He'd never been in a race; he had just run. But suddenly he found that he was very eager to win. It was as the Latin Master had said: there is a competitive instinct in man.

The winter months interrupted the rigorous training course Frank's friends had set for him. He found that he missed the physical exercise. He was restless, and it was difficult to keep his mind on his studies. But as soon as the spring winds dried up the roads, he was out again, and life took on new zest.

Finally the day of the meet arrived. Frank was nervous. The Second Formers were depending on him too much. There were Upper Form boys competing against him in the mile race, boys that were older and more experienced than he. He almost wished he'd never agreed to run, but he couldn't back out now. Dan and John and the others were counting on him.

The mile was to be run on a country road. The starting point was one section line; the finish line, another — the one that ran alongside of St. John's. There was a small knot of boys at the starting post, but Frank knew that most of his friends were waiting at the finish line.

The starter lined up the contestants. There were four of them running the mile, the other three all Upper Form boys. Frank drew the position on the far left. His heart was thumping as he put his toe on the line the starter had drawn in the dust, and crouched, waiting for the signal. He felt as he did on hunt mornings at home, and he was afraid this did not augur well for a successful race.

The moment was growing almost too tense to bear.
Then from behind him he heard the voice of the Latin
Master: " Good luck, Key. I'm betting on the Tenth
Legion."

Frank relaxed. He smiled. He stood up. " Thanks,"
he said. He took his position again. He felt much better.

" Ready! Get set! Go! "

They were off, and now Frank had no time to think.
All his faculties were concentrated on putting one foot in
front of the other smoothly, evenly. He and Dan and
John had agreed that he mustn't put too much into the
early part of the race. " Take it easy," Dan had said.
" Save your strength and your wind for a final push at
the finish." " Of course, you don't want to let the others
get too far ahead of you," John had cautioned. " You
might not be able to catch up."

The four ran very close at first. The boy to the far right
was slightly ahead. Frank and the boy immediately to his
right were neck and neck. The fourth was a mere pace
behind them.

Frank settled down to a steady gait. His lungs were filling evenly. This was where the training paid off! He
could no longer hear the group at the starting post. The
only sounds were the breathing of the boy beside him,
and the quiet country sounds that reminded him of home.

Suddenly he realized that the boy next to him was running much closer to him than he should be. He was being crowded, and he didn't like it. He felt hampered by
the lack of ample space for flailing arms and legs. Then
he saw that the boy was doing it on purpose. He was deliberately pushing him to the edge of the road. Frank's

fighting spirit rose. He wouldn't mind being beaten fair and square, but he wasn't going to be beaten by trickery. At the edge of the road the ground was rough. He didn't dare let himself be pushed out. He was still a long way from the finish line, but he put on a sudden burst of speed. Perhaps this would take his adversary by surprise.

With relief he saw that his strategy was working. In a matter of seconds, he shook his opponent from his right flank. At the same time he saw that he had also pulled almost abreast of the runner who had been out in front; but there was danger in this sudden spurt, and he knew it. It had already told on his wind. He tried to draw long breaths, and to get back into his earlier steady pace, but he had broken his stride, and it was difficult now to regain it.

Then he realized that the boy ahead of him was putting on more speed. The distance Frank had almost closed between the two widened rapidly. He looked ahead and saw the reason: the finish line was in sight. At least he saw a blur of people that indicated where it was, probably a quarter of a mile distant. This was the point at which he was supposed to begin his spurt of speed. He tried, but the only results were an ever-tightening constriction in his chest and a churning, jerky motion of his legs. It was no use. He'd put on his burst of speed too soon, and now he didn't have it. The figures that had looked small in the distance were growing larger. He had no time to waste. If he were to bring honor to the Second Form, it must be now. He tried harder, but he couldn't bring it off.

Suddenly he saw the flag waving over St. John's. It took

on a strange symbolism in his pounding brain. He was running to defend it. Do something for it besides fight, he had said, something besides fight your fellow man. All right, he was doing it. He was going to win this race!

He put everything he had into one final effort. His lungs seemed to be bursting, but he was gaining on the boy in the lead. The finish line was coming closer. They were almost upon it! He was even with the other boy. He

was past him! He was over the finish line!

He ran a little farther, slowing his stride, and when he stopped, Dan and John were beside him. Dan threw his jacket over his shoulders. One of them supported him on either side. " Keep walking," Dan said. " It was a great race, Key! A great race! "

Frank was having all he could do to catch his breath.

" Listen to the Second Formers yelling for you! " John cried.

" You won for us by a length."

" You make me sound like — a horse," Frank gasped.

" 'Ray, Key! 'Ray, Key! 'Ray, Key! " The yell struck his pounding eardrums fuzzily.

" Hear 'em? " Dan laughed exultantly. " You really put Second Form on the map. Good old boy! You won the mile for us."

" And for the flag," he murmured. He couldn't have explained what he meant, but he didn't have to. Dan and John didn't hear. They were too busy gloating over their victory.

7

FIRST LOVE

Frank didn't know where the years at St. John's had gone, but they were over. He was one of nineteen young men who had graduated from the college that June morning in 1796. As he bade the other members of the "Tenth Legion" good-by, there was a lump in his throat. Their lives had been close these past years. Now they were separating to go in as many and diverse directions as the spokes of a wheel, emanating from the hub that was St. John's.

John Shaw wanted to become a doctor. Dan Murray didn't know about the future. Frank would go home to Terra Rubra for the summer, then come back to Annapolis to read law in the fall. He had done considerable reading in his Uncle Philip's law library during his last year in college; he had sat in the gallery when the legislature was in session; he had studied the Constitution of the United States and that of Maryland. He felt that law was the thing for him.

He was surprised that Great-aunt Scott cried when he told her good-by. He hadn't realized how much it had meant to her to have him living in her home. He would not be returning to her, for he was to live at Uncle Philip's while he studied law. He put his arms around her slight little body and hugged her tight. " I'll come to see you, Aunt Scott, never fear."

He was riding home alone this time, and he was eager to be off. It would be something of an adventure to make the trip by himself, stopping overnight at his own choice of inns, making passing acquaintances as he desired.

Almost too soon the adventure was over, and he was nearing Terra Rubra.

" Terra Rubra, land of red earth,
  You have bound me to you from the day of my birth."

He smiled, remembering the lines he had written when he was preparing to leave Terra Rubra for the first time. But they were still true, despite the intervention of time and experience.

His pulses quickened as he began to sight familiar landmarks. There were the small German farms, neat as a garden you might draw on paper. There was Normand Bruce's quaint little white house on the hill overlooking the creek. And then at last the Big House itself, at Terra Rubra, the two wings fanning out at the rear like out-flung arms; back of it, the slave quarters, and beyond, the barns. He thought of his mother, still young and pretty; of his father, soft-spoken and gentle; of Ann, fun-loving and gay. He could hardly wait to see them all!

He spurred his horse. Now he was turning into the lane where he had first practiced his running. As he galloped up the lane, they heard him coming. Slaves came racing across the fields to be on hand to greet him. The front door of the house was thrown open and Ann and another girl ran out, followed by the household servants. But where were his mother and father?

" Welcome home, Massa Frank! "

" Massa Frank, we's got lots of questions to propound."

Frank waved his hat at them in greeting and jumped off his horse. He took Ann in his arms and swung her off her feet, then set her down and held her at arm's length. " Let me look at you! " he cried. " You get prettier every time I go away."

She laughed. " O Frank, I'm forgetting my manners. This is my friend Delia Storm. She lives down the road a piece. Her father bought the Reinbeck farm."

" Pleased, I'm sure," Frank said. He *was* pleased. Delia was little and plump and pretty. He smiled at her a long moment before he turned back to Ann. " Where are Mamma and Papa? " he asked his sister.

" Oh, Papa's off trying to get votes for the Democratic electors, and Mamma went with him to visit some of her old friends. Papa's at it all the time these days, traipsing all over the country."

Frank was interested at once. He himself was highly in favor of Jefferson. He'd be more than glad to help his father try to swing Frederick County for him. Uncle Philip was a strong Federalist, but he hadn't been able to influence his nephew politically. Frank believed as his father believed, that in a democracy the common man was important and must be given his chance.

" Will you-all be leadin' meetin' tonight, Massa Frank? " Mose asked, his good black face beaming.

" I'll be glad to, Mose. See you all then." He waved his

hat again, and the Negroes shambled back to work. Ever
since Frank could remember, his father had held evening
devotionals in the paved courtyard back of the house in
fair weather. He read from the Bible, said a prayer, and
led in the singing of a hymn. Since Frank had been attending college, his father had asked him to " lead meeting " when he was home.

Ann led the way into the house. " I doubt that Papa
and Mamma will be home tonight," she said. " That's
why Delia was going to stay with me. We didn't know for
sure when you'd get here."

" Perhaps now I shouldn't stay," Delia said shyly.

" Oh, yes, you must stay. We'll have so much fun with
Frank home."

" Stay, by all means," Frank said heartily. " I wouldn't
want you to leave just because I'm here. In fact," he
added, smiling at her, " I want you to stay because I'm
here."

Delia blushed and dropped her eyes, and Ann shot her
brother a quizzical look. Well, he was quite grown up.
There was no reason for her to be surprised at his evi-
dencing interest in a pretty girl.

At dinner, Delia was a good audience as Frank and Ann
reminisced and Frank told hilarious tales of escapades at
St. John's. The candlelight glowed softly on the ivory
damask cloth and the old silver. There's something so
intimate about a meal by candlelight, Frank thought. He
sat smiling at the girls, his blue eyes bright with happiness.

" Well, I promised Mose I'd conduct services," he said
at last. " I'd better go find something to read. You girls

will come out, won't you? "

" We'll be there," Ann promised.

He went into his father's study, took the big family Bible from the desk, and sat down in his father's easy chair. What a pleasant life his father led, he thought — the life of a country squire — his house the epitome of friendliness and hospitality, his position in the community one of esteem and love, his occupation varied and leisurely! It would be a good life. Was a law office in the city what he, Frank, wanted? His father had been admitted to the Bar and had been an associate district judge for years, riding about the country to sit in court in three counties over which he had jurisdiction. Why shouldn't he follow in his father's footsteps? There was his mother's cousin, Arthur Shaaf, with whom he could read law in nearby Frederick.

But he must quit daydreaming and find a passage of Scripture to read to the slaves. They would all be gathered in the court waiting for him. He opened the Book at random, and his eyes fell upon the words, " I will lift up mine eyes unto the hills, from whence cometh my strength." It was a passage he was fond of. He would read it, then talk briefly, using it as his text. His father usually read a longer passage on weekdays and left the sermon for Sunday morning. But he knew that the black folk would be eager for words from him. They thought he knew everything, now that he'd been to college.

Frank spoke simply but fluently. " Amens " from his audience punctuated his remarks. He glanced at Ann and Delia. Delia was watching him with a rapt expression, her lips parted. She's as pretty as a picture, he thought.

When the meeting was over, Ann and Delia joined him.

"Let's take a walk," Frank said. "It's full moon to-night. You girls don't know how wonderful it is to rediscover June in the country after you've been living in the city."

"I'd like a chance to find out," Ann said. "I don't

know when I've been to Annapolis! "

" I never have," Delia said.

" Haven't you really? " Frank asked, looking down at her.

She shook her head. " I've never been out of Frederick County," she said.

" Why, what a little innocent you are! " Frank exclaimed. He was walking between the two girls, a hand on the arm of each. Delia's arm was soft and warm. He thought he was going to have a very pleasant summer.

Nor was he wrong in his surmise. As the long, lazy summer days slipped by, Ann found herself more and more alone. She had soon begun to beg off when Frank and Delia tried to include her on their rambles through the woods or their boat trips on Pipe Creek, for she felt like a third thumb. She couldn't help envying Delia a little. What would it be like to be in love?

Frank felt guilty at first, leaving Ann out. But he soon became so absorbed in Delia and his own emotions that he had room for nothing else. He couldn't cven talk to Ann about it. How could you talk to people about being in love unless they had been in love? When he wasn't with Delia, he sat by the hour in front of his desk writing her poems. He was tremendously flattered by her praise of them. No one else had ever thought his poetry wonderful. Ann had taken it for granted; she could turn out a rhyme as easily as he. His friend John Shaw, who was the class poet, had criticized it severely.

More and more, as the summer went on, Frank's plans for the future shifted before his eyes. What could be more pleasant than to marry Delia and stay on at Terra Rubra, study law with Cousin Arthur, and take up his father's way of life — perhaps as a justice of the peace? But something kept him from discussing the matter with Delia.

" How soon are you going back to Annapolis? " she asked wistfully one afternoon as they paddled idly up Pipe Creek.

" I don't know," he said, feeling a touch of sadness. " Uncle Philip's expecting me in the fall. Perhaps I'll stay home till after the fox-hunting."

" Oh, I hope you do! "

" Do you, little Delia? " he asked softly. " You know that if I stay, it will be because of you."

That evening at dinner his father said: " Frank, would you like to go electioneering with me tomorrow? I'm going over west of Frederick."

" Of course, Papa," Frank said, but his heart sank. He and Delia had planned a picnic for tomorrow. What was the matter with him? When he had first come home, he had been eager to go with his father to secure votes for Jefferson. Now he begrudged spending even one day away from Delia. Still, if he went to Frederick, there might be an opportunity to talk to Cousin Arthur. Perhaps he could also broach the subject of a change of plans to his father.

" I had a letter from your Uncle Philip yesterday," his father said as they started out the next morning.

" What did he say? "

" He thinks it's time you're getting back to Annapolis. He said he had arranged with Judge Jeremiah Chase for you to study in his office. The judge takes only a few young men on each year, and he won't hold a place for you indefinitely, Philip says."

" Uncle Philip's gone that far? "

" Of course. You were expecting him to make arrangements for you, weren't you? "

" Yes, but — " Frank hesitated. This would be as good
a time as any to say what he'd been thinking. " Well, I've
been wondering if I wouldn't rather study law with
Cousin Arthur in Frederick than to go back to Annapolis — — "

" That, I should say, depends on what you want to do
with your life," his father said slowly.

Frank did not think he sounded pleased.

" What could be better than what you've done with
yours? " he said defensively. " I could go on living at
Terra Rubra, and get a judgeship one day."

His father said nothing. They rode in silence, and the
soft thud of the horses' hoofs in the dust was the only
sound.

After a time his father spoke. " Yes, Son, it's been a
good life, but I don't think it's for you. You've always
been ambitious. From the time you were a little fellow,
I've watched you and thought, ' Frederick County isn't
big enough for him.' You have too much ability, Frank.
You're like your Uncle Philip in some ways. I'm just an
ordinary man leading an ordinary existence. I think the
world holds something extraordinary for you, because I
think you have something extraordinary to give. That's
why I can't approve of this line of thought you're taking.
I don't think you'd ever be satisfied to settle down here.
I'm a judge, yes, but a little one. I deal with petty cases
and, what's worse, with petty minds. I think you would

find such a life deadly."

Frank didn't answer. All he could think about was the pain of parting from Delia.

" I think we'd better write Philip that you'll be back the first of October. If we give him a definite date, the judge will probably hold a place for you. You can try it until Christmas. Then if you still want to come back and study with Cousin Arthur, I won't stand in your way. But I don't think you'd be giving yourself a fair chance if you stayed now. A young man's judgment can get badly befuddled by a pretty face sometimes."

Frank had to smile. So his father had known what was at the bottom of his thinking all the time! Well, his proposition was fair enough. He was only asking him to stay away three months. He could hardly refuse. And there *was* his father's argument that he would have greater opportunities elsewhere. If it should mean greater opportunity to do something worth-while for his country and his flag — Well, he would see.

8

BACK TO THE CITY

Without argument, Frank was complying with his father's request that he return to Annapolis until Christmas, but he wasn't happy about going.

It was his last day at home. Delia was coming for dinner, and afterward, when he had walked home with her across the hills, he must say good-by. Already he felt the pain of parting. Then too he had drifted back into the pleasant ways of the family's life at Terra Rubra, and it was hard to pull away.

" Mamma," he said, going into the dining room where his mother was arranging a bouquet of autumn flowers, " let me borrow your diamond ring, will you? "

" Whatever for? " his mother asked in surprise, lifting her face above the orange and yellow blossoms so that their reflection cast a golden light on her cheek.

She sounded so taken aback that Frank laughed. " I just said ' borrow.' I didn't ask you to *give* it to me! "

" She probably thought you wanted it to give to somebody else," Ann put in mischievously.

" No comments from you, my dear sister! By the time I get back, *you'll* probably be wearing a diamond ring."

" I don't know where I'd get it," Ann laughed.

" What do you want with my ring, Frank? " his mother repeated, pulling it from her finger and holding it out to him.

" I want to use it for a cutting tool."

He took it and stepped to the window. Ann followed and watched over his shoulder as he started to scratch a " J " on the glass. He followed it with an " R " and then a " K."

" Papa's initials! " Ann cried.

Frank went on with his work, and his mother also came to watch.

Next he carved her initials. He was doing the letters in script.

" Very pretty," his mother said, " but isn't it a bit childish to be marking up the windowpane? "

Frank smiled, but went on working. Ann's initials came next. " I know you don't really mind, Mamma, or I wouldn't be doing it."

They could see now that he was placing the initials to form an arc. After Ann's came his own. " And now Uncle Philip's," he said, " and we'll have the family circle. I just wanted to leave some tangible evidence of the way I feel about the Key family. It doesn't make any difference whether we agree or disagree on politics or careers or whatever; we're a family circle with no break in the circle, and we always will be, no matter what happens."

Ann looked at him quizzically. She had a feeling he meant something in particular. Had he spoken to Papa about Delia and met with disapproval?

He stood back to survey his handiwork. " Ann," he

said, " where's that old silver pitcher that has the family coat of arms on it? "

" Oh, dear, I don't know. Where is it, Mamma? "

" It's in that sideboard there."

" Get it for me, will you? " Frank said. " I'd like to put the family coat of arms in the center of my circle. I need a pattern."

Ann brought the pitcher and held the side with the coat of arms toward the light. Roughly, Frank sketched a griffin's head holding a large key in its beak as it appeared on the pitcher.

" The griffin, according to Greek mythology — "

" The learned college man speaks," Ann twitted him.

Frank went on as if he had not been interrupted — " is the guardian of man and his earthly possessions. So may the griffin guard the Key family and Terra Rubra while we are apart."

" A pretty design and a pretty sentiment, Son," his mother said. Frank could tell by the smile in her eyes that she was pleased with his symbolism.

Life in Annapolis, living at Uncle Philip's and reading law, proved to be very different from what it had been when he was living at Great-aunt Scott's and attending St. John's. Uncle Philip had married the governor's daughter, and their home was the scene of just such gay and frequent parties as Ann had once said she imagined at their uncle's. Frank soon found himself enjoying the round of parties. He thought less and less longingly of the quiet country life he had lived during the summer. At first he wrote Delia long letters, telling her everything

he did, but the letters he received in return soon ceased
to interest him, and he wrote less and less frequently.
Gradually the image of Delia faded.

By Christmas time he had almost forgotten his father's
stipulation that he need stay in Annapolis only until
Christmas. He was surprised to get a letter from Terra
Rubra asking whether he planned to stay or return home.
He sat down at his desk at once to answer.

" Dear Father," he wrote. " First of all I want to thank
you for advising me to come back to Annapolis. I guess I
was in a haze last summer, as I think you suspected, and
wasn't seeing straight.

" I am very happy with Uncle Philip, feel that I am
progressing splendidly with Judge Chase, and wouldn't
consider giving up my studies here.

" I will surely try to make a place for myself in the law
that will warrant your being proud of me.

" Your loving son,
" Frank."

Smiling to himself, he folded the letter and put it in an
envelope. How could he have thought, three brief months
ago, that he would be content to marry Delia and settle
down as a country lawyer? He sealed the letter and went
out to post it. As he reached the street, he met a slight
young man, hands in pockets and shoulders hunched
against the cold, hurrying toward him.

" Taney! " he exclaimed. " Coming to see me? Fine!
I'm just going to the corner to post this letter. Will you
come along? "

" I'll go in and wait if you don't mind. I'm freezing."

" Do that. Go up to my study. I'll be back in a jiffy."

He hurried to finish his errand. It was like Taney to come out with too light a coat, then shiver in the cold. He was as impractical as he was brilliant. Of the six young men who were studying with Judge Jeremiah Townley Chase, Taney was Frank's favorite. It was strange, he mused, how their friendship had sprung up. They were as different as two people could be. Taney was a Federalist, Frank a Democrat; Taney was a Roman Catholic, Frank a Protestant; Taney took his law study very seriously, Frank took his lightly; Taney wasted no time in society, Frank spent many of his evenings " partying."

He took the stairs two at a time, eager to visit with his friend. " You know," he said, as he burst in to find Taney warming himself before the fire, " I think about the only thing you and I have in common is horses, yet I find you my most congenial companion. How do you account for that? "

Taney answered instantly. " We're both tolerant. We're both intelligent. Which means we can listen to the other fellow's point of view without thinking him a fool or becoming annoyed because he doesn't agree with us."

Frank laughed heartily. " You're always sure about things, aren't you, Taney? In that respect too I'm different. I just posted a letter to my father telling him I was perfectly content studying law with the Judge, and yet, there were doubts in my mind, even as I wrote the letter. I don't know whether I'm satisfied to make law the end view of my life."

" *I* have no doubts. The prospect of law as a career fascinates me. I can't learn enough, fast enough."

" H'm," Frank said. " I'd sensed that." He thought a minute then added, " I think I can truthfully say that the prospect of a career in law fascinates me also, but I'm not sure that it satisfies me."

" What is it you want? " Taney demanded.

Frank shook his head. " I guess I don't know. I've toyed with the idea of going into the seminary."

Taney eyed him speculatively. " What does your Uncle Philip think of that? "

" Just what you think he thinks: that there's no future in it. A future to Uncle Philip means fame and fortune."

" What does it mean to you? " Taney asked briskly.

" It's a little hard to say," Frank admitted. " I guess helping my fellow men and my country."

" Well, you can do that in the law," Taney said. That settled it. He was through with the discussion.

Frank smiled and changed the subject. " You know," he said, " I'd like very much to have you come visit us at Terra Rubra next summer. I'd like to have you see that we have beautiful horses and fine hunting in Frederick County."

" I'd like that," Taney said, his eyes bright.

" Then it's settled. When the Judge dismisses us for the summer, you'll go along home with me."

" I'll be very happy to."

Suddenly there was a loud knock, and before Frank could open the door, it burst open.

" Why, Dan! Dan Murray! " Frank exclaimed. " Come in. Meet Roger Taney. He's another of Judge Chase's protégés. Dan's an old St. John's friend, Taney. I'm glad to have you two meet."

" Why aren't you fellows downstairs? " Dan demanded. " Don't you know there are beautiful young ladies below? "

" Totally ignorant of the fact," Frank admitted. " Let's go."

" I'd better be getting on home," Taney demurred.

" Oh, you can't run off like this. Come on down. Who's here, Dan? "

" The Lloyds. The Colonel and his three beautiful daughters. Haven't you met them? "

" No, I think not."

" Then you have a treat coming. Prepare yourselves, men! "

Frank laughed, but he straightened his tie and brushed his hair.

They went down, but though there were three girls in the room, and Frank met them all, he saw only one. Her name was Mary Lloyd.

9

MARY LLOYD

Mary Lloyd was just four-
teen the night Frank met her. She wasn't like any other
girl he had ever known. He tried to analyze the difference after the guests had left and he had returned to his
room. How was she different? She was pretty, but so were
Ann and Delia. She was gay, but so were the other girls he
had gone skating and boating with. There was a dignity
about her, an aloofness, that set her apart even from her
sisters. Was that the quality that intrigued him? What
was she thinking, under her cap of bright curls, as she
watched the others with an inscrutable little smile?

He had tried to find out. " Do you like poetry? " he
had asked.

" Some poetry," she answered. Her hands were quiet
in her lap. His were creasing and recreasing the lace at
his cuffs.

" Do you like to ride? "

She nodded.

" Perhaps we could ride together some morning? "

" I'm not allowed to ride out with young gentlemen.
I'm only fourteen."

Standing before his mirror, Frank smiled a one-sided

smile. What had Uncle Philip said to him when he was
having trouble at St. John's because of his curly hair?
"The girls will swoon over you one of these days, with
that curly hair and blue eyes." Well, this girl certainly
hadn't swooned over him — even though he had let his
hair grow again. She had been completely indifferent to
his charms. But he would see her again. He would not let
the rebuffs of one evening stop him.

He did see her occasionally during the remainder of
the winter and through the spring. He saw her at a few
parties. He was invited once to the Lloyd home for dinner, with his uncle and aunt. But Mary gave no more in-
dication of swooning over him than she had at their first
meeting. In fact, Frank thought derisively, she doesn't
even act as if she knows I'm alive. What's the matter with
me? Am I so dull? She seems to like Dan Murray. At least
she talks to him, and that's more than she does to me.

Finally, one morning in early June, Judge Chase
spread his red robes and asked his peppery questions of
his six law students for the last time until fall.

"How would you brief this case, Key?" he asked
Frank. He had been outlining the facts of the case for
fifteen minutes, and Frank had not been listening. He
had been thinking about Mary Lloyd. Summer heat was
already bearing down on them, the Judge was wiping his
forehead, and Frank was prickling to be off to Terra
Rubra.

"I'm sorry, Sir. I lost you back there where you left
the history of the case and went into the technicality involved."

" A good lawyer has to learn to concentrate, Key; it's necessary to follow every word of the opposition. Taney? "

Taney knew what the Judge had said. He had already briefed the case in his mind. He gave it forth like a machine into which had been fed a raw product, out of which came a finished one. Frank marveled at him, as he had often done. He sighed. He was a little ashamed of himself for not giving the Judge closer attention. Judge Chase had shown him special consideration and had worked hard with him, because of Uncle Philip. He should be doing his part more conscientiously. The trouble was, there were so many other interesting things to think about!

" I'll see you in the fall when this beastly heat is over," the Judge said, dismissing them. " Good-by, Taney. Good-by, Key."

" Good-by, Sir," Frank said, extending his hand. He smiled his charming smile. " And I will try to do better in the fall. I want you to know I appreciate your efforts with me."

He hurried down the steps to catch Taney. " How early can you be ready in the morning? " he asked.

" Whenever you say."

" Four o'clock? "

Taney looked sidewise at him. " I thought you'd probably have to be up all hours tonight telling Mary Lloyd good-by."

Frank laughed ruefully. " Not a chance," he said. " ' I'm only fourteen,' " he mimicked. " ' I'm not al-

lowed to stay up and talk to young men.' Well, I've one
consolation. By the time I get back in the fall, she'll be
fifteen."

Taney laughed. " You're persistent, and not easily discouraged — good traits in a lawyer, my friend! "

All the way home to Terra Rubra, Frank wondered
about Delia. Would she expect to pick up where they had
left off last summer? Or would she realize that his ceasing
to write meant that he had lost interest? He hated the
thought of being cruel. He did hope she would not be at
Terra Rubra when he arrived, but if she were, at least
he had Taney with him as a foil. He had been living an
idyll last summer. It seemed now like a pleasant dream;
he must have been in a half-somnolent state. Everything
had had an indefinable shape, blending into the soft,
dreamy summer days as objects cease to have outline in
the mist.

Now everything was in sharp focus in his mind. There
were straight lines and sharp corners. He would go back
to Annapolis in the fall with two definite goals before
him: To succeed at the law as Uncle Philip wanted him
to, and to marry Mary Lloyd and give her the kind of life
she was used to. He would work as hard at the law as at
courting Mary and vice versa. He was determined to succeed at both.

Frank was pleased at his friend Taney's obvious pleasure in the Redlands as they neared Terra Rubra. " Why,
it's beautiful country! " Taney exclaimed.

" What did you expect? " Frank asked. " Barren red
hills, bald as Judge Chase's head? "

" I guess I hadn't realized how productive the west-

ern counties were — all these fields of flax and buckwheat — "

" We're patriotic in Frederick County," Frank said.
" See that red plowed field, then the field of buckwheat
with its white bloom, and the blue field of flax? The red,
the white, and the blue."

Taney glanced at him. " Funny how close the flag always is to the foreground of your consciousness," he said.

Frank shrugged. " A fellow has to have something that's
important to him. With you it's the law — "

" With you it had better be the law too! You know, I
miss seeing tobacco fields."

Frank laughed. " In the days when my grandfather
founded Terra Rubra, they did grow tobacco hereabouts.
But it was as bitter as gall, and as soon as they had roads
so they could bring tobacco in, they gave up growing it.
There's something in the soil — — "

" Brick dust, by the looks of it," Taney interrupted,
grinning.

They rode on in companionable silence. It was a
bright, clear day, and Frank was glad. There was a view
he wanted Taney to see from the next hill, and this was
the right kind of day to do it justice.

" Let's rein up a minute when we get to the top of the
hill," he said. Taney nodded and followed Frank's ex-
ample when he drew up at the crest of the hill and turned
his horse's head to the north.

Frank didn't say a word. He watched Taney's face.
Taney didn't say anything, either, but he let out a low
whistle. In the distance rose two blue mountains, round
and symmetrical. " Little Round Top and Big Round

Top," Frank said. " They always make me think of one nice, fat biscuit that came out just right and one that puffed up too high."

" You're a born poet, Key," Taney said. " The fields remind you of the flag, the mountains of biscuits. To me they're just fields and mountains. Beautiful, it's true, but still fields and mountains."

When they arrived at Terra Rubra, Frank was relieved to find only the family there to greet them. " Ann, I want to present my friend Roger Taney."

" Oh, I've heard so much about you in Frank's letters — it's as if I'd known you forever," Ann chattered. " Only I didn't know you were so thin. Goodness! We'll have to fatten you up while you're here."

Frank chuckled, seeing how Taney smiled on Ann. Usually his friend was shy with girls, but with Ann he seemed at ease.

Frank took Ann aside after dinner when his father had Taney engaged in a political discussion. " Didn't I tell you you'd like him? " he said.

" You did, and I do," Ann retorted gaily.

" Now, what about Delia? "

" What about Mary? " Ann countered, her eyes dancing.

" I haven't made the slightest headway," Frank confessed. " I'm not over the first little pebble of the mountain that looms between us, but she's the girl I'm going to marry."

" My, what egotism! " Ann laughed.

" Don't laugh at me. I'm deadly serious. Now what about Delia? I hope she isn't — isn't counting on anything from me. You're her friend; you surely know."

Ann couldn't resist keeping him in suspense. " When little boys play with fire, they should expect to get their fingers scorched, shouldn't they? "

Frank looked at her out of frightened eyes. " But, Ann," he protested, " I — I didn't mean anything by it. I mean — Well, at the time, maybe I did, but I didn't say so. I don't want to hurt her."

Then Ann laughed. " You don't need to worry," she said. " Delia's already married to one of the German boys over west of Frederick."

Frank let out a long sigh of relief. " Thank goodness! " he said.

He and Ann walked back into the parlor. Taney dropped his political discussion and jumped up.

" Won't you sit here, Miss Ann? " he asked, indicating a place beside him on the horsehair love seat under the window.

Mr. Key turned to Frank. " Would you and your friend like to go into Frederick with me tomorrow? The Federalists are having a gathering, and I like to get the tenor of their meetings. The better we know their strength, the better we can prepare to defeat them."

" Taney will add one to their strength if we take him along," Frank laughed. " He's a Federalist, you know."

" So I have discovered."

" Well, so's Uncle Philip," Ann spoke up defensively. " I guess there's nothing wrong with being a Federalist."

Frank and his father laughed. " Who said there was? " Frank asked.

" Would you like to go? " Mr. Key repeated.

"How about it, Taney?" Frank asked.

"I'd like to if you would."

"Why does it have to be such an exclusively masculine party?" Ann asked. "I need to go into Frederick, don't I, Mamma? To get the trim for my new dress."

Mrs. Key smiled. "If your father doesn't mind —"

Ann was with them when they set out for Frederick the next day. In fact, Ann and Taney were riding in the carriage, Frank and his father on horseback.

"Your friend and your sister seem to have taken a rapid fancy to each other," Mr. Key said to Frank with a smile.

"I'm glad," Frank said, "Ann being my favorite sister and Taney my favorite friend!"

As they rode into the outskirts of Frederick, they could hear singing. " That's the Federalists' new song," Mr. Key said. " It will do more toward re-electing Adams than all the speeches in the country."

" Oh? " said Frank. " I haven't heard it. What is it? "

" ' Adams and Liberty.' It praises the President's firm notes to France and England."

" It's a rousing tune," Frank said, as they drew closer to the Square.

His father nodded. " It's an old tune — ' To Anacreon in Heaven ' — but with the ' Adams and Liberty ' words it makes a very spirited campaign song."

Frank found himself whistling the tune on the way home.

Taney leaned out of the carriage and called to him, "The Federalists have got you! "

" It's not the Federalists. It's the tune," Frank called back.

10

"TO MARY"

You're going at your studies as if you meant business this fall," Uncle Philip said. He had joined Frank in his upstairs study one evening and was sprawled in an easy chair watching Frank at his desk.

" I do mean business," Frank said. He had been poring over a case, and he marked his place with a pencil before giving his full attention to his uncle.

" I'm glad of it," Uncle Philip said. " I'd like to talk to you if you can spare a few minutes."

Frank nodded.

" This may come as a surprise to you, but I think my days of practicing law in Annapolis are about over."

Frank was surprised. His uncle was admittedly the leading lawyer in Annapolis. " What do you mean? " he said.

" I'm thinking ahead. I've gone as far as I can here. I'm looking for greener pastures."

Frank had supposed that his uncle would spend the rest of his days in Annapolis, and he had fully expected to be asked to go into practice with him when he was admitted to the Bar. In fact, he thought he and his uncle had always had such a tacit understanding. So this an-

nouncement **came as a** blow. He thought at once of
Mary Lloyd.

" I'm thinking about the new Capital," Uncle Philip
went on.

" You mean you're thinking of moving to Washington? " Frank asked in amazement. Everything he had
heard about the crude frontier settlement which was the
country's new capital would have led him to believe that
his uncle would want to stay as far away from it as possible. Just the other week, the United States Senator from
Maryland had been a guest of Uncle Philip's and had re-
galed the family at dinner with stories of the President's
getting stuck in the mud between his house and the
Capitol, of the Supreme Court Justices swatting flies as
they heard cases, and of —— ——

Supreme Court Justices! Suddenly the picture came
clear in Frank's mind. His uncle was going to get near
the base of operations. He wanted to be close to the highest court in the land. Uncle Philip's ambition never
ceased to awe him. He sat staring at his uncle.

Something of his dawning understanding must have
shown in his face, for his uncle said: " Yes, I'm thinking
about getting in on the ground floor. Washington is raw
and unattractive now, but it is very young. It won't stay
that way forever. Besides, the important thing isn't what
you see out the front door of your house, but what you
see in the front door of your office."

" I see what you mean," Frank said. But he was still dis-
turbed over the implications to his own future. Did Uncle
Philip expect him to come to Washington too? He wasn't
at all sure that he wanted to. The miserable frontier life

of the Capital did not sound like the kind of life he could ask Mary to share with him. Or wouldn't Uncle Philip have a place for him in Washington? He would be pioneering. Things wouldn't be the same as in Annapolis where his practice was flourishing and munificent.

" Now about you," his uncle said. " I suppose you were expecting to settle here. And if I'm not mistaken, there's a certain young lady in the picture." He smiled. " So my plans may come as something of a blow to you. I'm sorry, if that's the case, but I believe in the long run my move will be to the advantage of both of us."

Then he is expecting me to join him in Washington, Frank thought. He was taken by surprise at his uncle's next words.

" I think," he said, " that you should have a little experience before you come to Washington; that is, provided you want to come in with me in the Capital, which I hope you will. It's going to be the best place in the country for a talented young lawyer to practice. But I doubt if it would be wise for me to take you on at once. How soon do you expect to finish your studies? "

" I'm planning to take the examinations in the spring."

" So I thought. Then I would suggest that you find a place with a practiced law firm for this coming year. By the following one, I should be well enough established in the Capital to take you on, and you should have gained enough experience to be of some value to me. Think it over."

Frank thought it over. He could think of nothing else. He gave up trying to make sense of the case he was reading. His greatest concern was: How will Mary fit into this new picture? Obviously, of course, the first thing was to win her. So far his advances had met with complete indifference, as far as he could see.

He picked up his pencil, and the lines of a poem grew on the paper before him, on which he had intended briefing a law case:

TO MARY

Frown on, ye dark and angry clouds;
And, Winter, blow that blast again,
That calls thy wrathful host to pour
Their fury on the wasted plain.

'Tis thus I choose my way to win
To her whose love my bosom warms;
And brighter seems the prize I seek,
Seen through the gloom of clouds and storms.

Let colder lovers shrink from these,
And calmly wait for peaceful skies;
Be mine, through toil and pain to win
The beams of Mary's gladdened eyes.

Perhaps she'll value more my love,
Perhaps give more of hers to me,
Perhaps may greet me with a smile
More sweet, if smile more sweet can be.

O Mary, couldst thou know this heart,
Could words or deed its truth declare,
'Twould higher raise love's flame in thine,
Or light it, if it be not there!

There, that should let her know plainly enough how he felt. He would go post it.

Two days later as he left the courtroom where Judge Chase's students had been listening to a trial, he decided to walk by the Lloyds'. Mary should have received his poem yesterday in the post. He would follow it up with a personal call.

As he rang the bell at the beautiful old Samuel Chase mansion, which the Lloyds had bought when Judge Samuel Chase left Annapolis for a position on the Supreme Court, his spirits were up again. Now that he'd had time to absorb the impact of his uncle's plans, they sounded good to him. He believed they would inure to his advantage ultimately, and certainly they would give him greater opportunity to be of service to his country. He found himself wanting to fall in with them, but it would all depend on Mary. At the moment, he even felt optimistic about her. Judge Chase had complimented him on the way he had seen through the mass of evidence to the core of the case just tried, and he felt as if the world were his.

The massive door of the Lloyd house, with its heavy ornamental brass knocker, swung inward, and the Lloyd butler stood staring at Frank in surprise.

" Good afternoon, Tom. Is Miss Mary in? "

" Laws yes, Massa Key. She's in, all right. They's all in, but not presentable. They's all aflutterin' an' afumin', fixin' up for tonight's ball."

Frank had forgotten about the Murrays' ball. He would see Mary there tonight. But he knew from experience that he would do well to get one dance with her. He felt a sudden longing to see her alone. Now that he was here, he wasn't going to retreat.

" Will you tell her I'd like to see her, please? " he said, walking past the colored man at the door.

" I'll tell her, Massa Key, but I don't think she kin see you."

" Tell her just to come down as she is. I want to speak with her only a minute."

Tom disappeared, and Frank wondered, if she did come down, what he could say to her that would warrant his insistence upon seeing her. I'll make up something about tonight, he decided. I'll tell her I have to come late, and that I want her to save a dance for me.

He was sitting on the edge of a stiff chair in the parlor, holding his hat in his hand and telling himself he was a fool for coming, when he heard the unmistakable click of feminine heels in the hall. Had Mary come down, or had she sent one of her sisters in her place?

He jumped up, his heart pounding, his eyes on the door. In another instant, it opened, and Mary stood framed in the mellow, late-afternoon light. He couldn't speak. He took a step toward her as she came across the room to him, talking as she came.

" Mr. Key," she said, " you are most importune, calling on a young lady at this hour of the day when you know she is preparing to attend a ball."

" I'm sorry, Mary. I'd forgotten about the Murrays' ball." He had also forgotten the excuse he had planned. Now he had spoiled everything. Her hair was pulled back from her forehead and rolled in curl papers all over her head. She looked more of a child than ever. She looked adorable. He smiled at her.

"What do you want?" she demanded bluntly.

"I — I — " Frank stammered. Then he remembered his poem. "I was just wondering if you got my poem."

She laughed, and there was real mirth in the laugh.

He looked at her in surprise. He hadn't thought the poem was funny.

"I got it," she said, "and I'm making very good use of it."

Frank's brows drew together. *How* did one make use of a love poem?

"See?" she said, her voice tinkling with laughter. She came closer and leaned her head toward him. "I didn't have enough curl papers for Amanda to put all my hair up, so we tore up your poem and used it."

Frank didn't know whether to be angry or amused at her. Well, it was a good joke on him. He laughed.

"Thank you, Mr. Key," she said with a little curtsy that made the curl papers rattle. "For your help, I will give you a dance tonight. And now you really must excuse me, or I shall never be ready for the ball."

Frank sighed ruefully as the door closed behind him. If he hadn't been convinced before that Mary had no sentimental feelings toward him or his poetry, he should be now! But at least he would have a dance with her tonight.

11

FIRST HURDLES

Frank and Taney were pounding each other on the back.

"We passed! We passed!" Frank cried. "We're members of the Maryland Bar. Francis Scott Key and Roger Brooke Taney, Attorneys at Law!"

"I wish it was as easy as that," said Taney, always less given to enthusiasms than Frank.

"So do I," Frank said, sobering, "I have to get busy and find a place that will give me the experience Uncle Philip insists on before he takes me in."

Taney sighed. "You're lucky to have an uncle to take you in," he said.

"I know I am. I wish he'd have room for both of us."

"No such luck," Taney said, shaking his head.

"I'm not sure, though, that I want to go in with Uncle Philip," Frank suddenly confessed. It was the first time he had ever voiced the thought, and it sounded both ungrateful and improbable.

"Have you lost your wits?" Taney demanded.

"Probably," Frank admitted. They were passing a little café which they had frequented during their years

with Judge Chase. " Let's go in and have a cup of coffee,"
he said.

They sat at their usual round table, draped with its red-
and-white checked cloth, and Taney picked up the conversation where they had left it. " I suppose you mean
Mary might not want to go to Washington."

Frank nodded. " I'm having a hard enough time," he
said ruefully, " without adding that handicap."

" She likes you," Taney said. " She's just young and
wants to go her own way for a while, like a colt that
hasn't been broken."

Frank laughed. " I can break any colt in Maryland,"
he said, " but I don't seem to know the proper procedure
where young women are concerned."

" Give her time to grow up," Taney advised.

They had finished their coffee. As they rose to go,
Frank said: " I'm over one hurdle, even though it is a
low one. She calls me Frank now and lets me call her
Polly."

Taney stopped stock-still and whistled. " You're doing all right," he said. " I'm not going to worry any more
about you. I heard your Mary throw a regular tantrum
when Dan Murray called her Polly one night. She said
positively no one outside the family was permitted to
call her Polly."

A broad smile spread over Frank's face. There had
been a time when he thought Mary favored Dan over
him.

After a month of seeking a place in a law firm, Frank
was thoroughly discouraged. The old established firms
either wanted no " young upstarts," as one lawyer told

him, or they would pay only a pittance that no one could live on. And now that he had been admitted to the Bar, he was determined to make his own way. He knew that if he wrote his father the situation, he would continue his allowance, but he didn't want that. What he wanted was to feel himself a man, independent of his father's support, able to take his place in the world.

He debated a long time before he went to see Mary. He was in no position to ask her to marry him, nor was he sure that he had won her to the point of saying, " Yes." But he did want to talk this over with her. He wrote a note asking her to go boating with him on the Severn Sunday afternoon. He even went so far as to say it was important that he talk to her, though he wondered if this were wise. He didn't want to frighten her off.

He had a pleasant surprise when he called for her.

" I had Mandy fix us a lunch," she said, indicating a basket on the hall table, covered with a snowy-white napkin. " I thought we could find a pretty, grassy spot and have a picnic."

Frank was delighted. It was the first time she had done anything to further his efforts in courting her. " Wonderful! " he exclaimed.

" I have to run get my parasol. I'll just be a minute. I think Papa's in here in the parlor." She led him to the door, and Colonel Lloyd rose from his easy chair, newspaper in hand.

" It's nice to see you, Frank," he said. " A fine day for young folks to be out on the river." He smiled.

" Thank you, Sir." Even the Colonel seemed more friendly than usual.

" Have you found a place? " he asked.

Frank felt embarrassed. " No, I haven't, Sir," he said.

To his relief, Mary came back into the room just then. She was looking even prettier than usual. She was wearing a pink-sprigged muslin dress and swinging a little pink parasol.

" Have a good time, children," the Colonel said. " Take good care of her, Frank."

"You can rest assured I will, Sir."

The day was hot, but when they reached the river, with the willows on the bank spreading their shade over the water and a little breeze ruffling the surface, it was pleasant. As Frank rowed downstream, he was filled with content. Mary chatted amiably, and he listened, happy in the sound of her voice and in her nearness.

" There's a pretty place, Frank," Mary said after a time.

Frank beached the boat and they climbed out. Mary spread a cloth on the grass and put out their supper. Only after they were happily full of fried chicken and biscuits and green-apple pie, did Frank broach the subject that was on his mind.

" Your father asked me if I'd found a place yet," he began.

" Have you? " Mary asked.

Frank's heart beat harder, for the tone of her voice made it sound as if she cared. He shook his head. " No, I haven't — at least nothing that I want. That's what I wanted to talk to you about. I'm thinking of going home."

" To Terra Rubra? "

There was unmistakable concern in her voice, and Frank knew both gladness and sorrow.

" Yes," he said. " My mother's cousin has the leading law practice in Frederick, and he's suggested several times that I come in with him. I wanted to stay here — because you're here, Polly." He paused and looked at her. She was sitting on the grass, her full skirts spread about her, facing him across the white lunch cloth. She had been watching his face earnestly, but now her eyes fell. " That's what I wanted to talk to you about," he went on. " I don't know whether I should go or stay — " He left it hanging, a half question between them.

Mary still didn't look up. " I think that's for you to decide, Frank," she said.

Frank sighed. " I suppose it is," he admitted. " But it's hard, Polly. You know how I would hate to leave you, yet if it's for the best interests of my future, perhaps — — " He didn't want to say too much. " Perhaps, for both our sakes, I should go."

Frank didn't think it was the rosy light of the sunset that suddenly suffused Mary's face. " Perhaps you should, Frank," she said very low.

" I'd come to see you just as often as I could get away."

She raised her head then, and the old saucy, teasing look was in her eyes. " If I'd let you! " she said, laughing.

Frank laughed too, his happiness and relief bubbling over. " You pixie! " he said. Then he turned serious. " But you would let me come, wouldn't you, Polly? I couldn't bear to go away from you if I thought — — "

" If you wanted to come to Annapolis to see your friends, I'm sure I wouldn't stand in your way," she said with mock primness.

" Then I think I'd better go, Polly, but I'll be back

for a visit before snow flies."

"The way it looks today, that won't be very soon."

Frank was sure there was a note of wistfulness in her voice. "I didn't say how long before snow flies," he said.

He stood up and held out a hand to her. "Come on. We'd better be getting back. I told your father I'd take good care of you, and that means getting off the river before the mists settle." He wouldn't mention Washington and Uncle Philip yet. One step at a time. If he could come back to see her often, during his apprenticeship with Cousin Arthur, he would be content. He would cross the other bridge when he reached it.

Frank went home to Terra Rubra. He explained to Cousin Arthur that if he came in with him in Frederick, it would be only a temporary arrangement. Cousin Arthur was satisfied. "I'll be happy to have you with me for the year," he said. "If you want to stay longer, I'll be glad to have you do that too. But I understand how it is with a young man. He wants to go where there is the greatest future, and I think your uncle is right about Washington."

He lived at home and rode back and forth to Frederick. He enjoyed being at home, and he enjoyed his work. But he was most impatient for an excuse to get back to Annapolis. What if Polly should again turn an interested ear to Dan Murray or some of the other young men at hand, now that he was not there to take her to parties or on excursions? He confided his fears in Ann.

"She'd be a fool not to wait for you," Ann said, smiling at him in admiration. "Look at yourself in the glass once in a while. There's no handsomer young man in Annapolis, I'm sure. You're talented; you have a future. You're generous and kindhearted. What more could a girl ask? "

Frank sighed. " Perhaps that I be on hand," he said. " If I only knew — "

He was overjoyed when one morning in October he entered the office to find Cousin Arthur poring over a letter which he said gave them cause for going to Annapolis — one of them. " Which shall it be? " he asked, his eyes twinkling.

" I'll be glad to go, Cousin Arthur," Frank said quickly.

Cousin Arthur allowed himself an amused chuckle. " When can you go? "

" Any time. Tomorrow — today — at once! "

" Well, there's a bit of preliminary work to be done on this," he said. " But I think we should be able to get it shaped up today so you could leave tomorrow."

" Thank you, Cousin Arthur." He could hardly keep his voice steady, and his heart was jumping like a jack rabbit. Just today, plus eighty miles, lay between him and Polly!

12

BAD LUCK AND GOOD

Frank started out in high spirits the next morning. How often he had covered the miles between Terra Rubra and Annapolis! His horse knew the way as well as he did. He amused himself by making up verses; it helped to pass the hours. Occasionally the autumn scene through which he was riding inspired the words for a poem, but more often it was Mary.

As the sun sank in the west, a great glowing bushel basket of fire that spilled red coals to right and left, Frank began to lay his plans for the night. Ordinarily he stopped about sundown, but tonight he had decided to press on. He knew the road so well; why shouldn't he continue after dark? Instead of stopping at the Pig and Whistle as usual, he would go on to the Highland. Comet could easily travel another two hours. He was so eager to get to Annapolis and Mary that he could not bear to think of wasting the evening hours sitting in an inn listening to political arguments.

The air grew chill after the sun went down. He pulled his coat collar up about his ears and spoke words of encouragement to his horse. " It won't be long now till you'll have your supper. In another hour we should be

at the Highland. It's been a long day, but tomorrow we'll see Polly."

Suddenly Comet began to shy.

"What's the matter, boy?" Frank said. And then he knew. Out of the darkness at the side of the road loomed three shadowy figures. Before he had time to think, one had grabbed his horse's bridle and the other two had pulled him from the saddle. His arms were pinioned behind him, but he struggled desperately to free himself. From the time he had made this trip as a schoolboy at St. John's, his father had insisted that he carry a pistol for just such an emergency as this. But he could not wrench his arm free to get at it. As he struggled, he felt a sudden, sharp blow on his head, and he knew no more.

When he came to, it was to a throbbing pain in his head and the knowledge that Comet was standing over him. Painfully, he tried to sit up. Every bone in his body cried out. They must have done a thorough job of beating me, he thought. Why wasn't that blow on the head enough? He sat with his head in his hands for a long moment, trying to clear the dizziness from his brain. Then he felt for his pistol. It was gone, of course. He felt for his money belt. It too was gone. — Well, I guess it's what I get for trying to push on after dark. I've been warned often enough. Now what do I do? The Pig and Whistle

would trust me for a night's lodging, but what about
the Highland?

It was too far to go back to the place where he was
known. He would have to risk being taken in at the Highland. He was stiff with the cold. Comet nuzzled his shoulder, and he reached for the bridle. The horse neighed
softly as if to give him encouragement. Little by little he
pulled himself up and stood against the horse's side,
steadying himself before he tried to mount. Finally he
put a foot in the stirrup and eased himself into the saddle. He groaned. " Take it easy, Comet."

The horse seemed to understand. He picked his way
carefully in the darkness. Frank was not conscious of the
miles, only of the pain. He would have passed the Highland without seeing it had Comet not stopped. Startled
by the cessation of motion, he blinked his eyes and saw
yellow squares of light before him. " The Highland," he
muttered. Painfully he slipped out of the saddle and
staggered toward the door. The door opened and a shaft
of light cut a wedge from the darkness.

" He's been beaten! " someone cried.

He leaned against the doorjamb and felt himself slip-
ping again into blessed oblivion.

This time when he regained consciousness, he was in
bed. As he opened his eyes, he saw a dim light burning
on a table in the corner of the room, but he did not at
once discover that someone was sitting in a chair beside
him. He reached a hand up to his head to touch the
bandage which encircled it.

" Feeling better? " a soft voice said.

He jumped and turned his head cautiously to see

where the voice had come from.

" I didn't mean to startle you." There was a woman sitting in a straight chair at his bedside.

" I didn't see you," he said thickly. " My head feels much better. Did you bandage it? "

" Indeed I did, after we'd washed you off. You were a bloody sight to behold! "

" It was very kind — "

" Never mind about that. Human beings wouldn't be much good if they couldn't help one another in time of need. You aren't the first victim of highwaymen that has staggered to our door. If only people would learn not to ride after night! "

" I know," Frank sighed. " I have no money," he added. " They took my pistol and my money belt."

The woman nodded. "My husband isn't afraid of being cheated out of his room rent. You have a fine horse, he says, and a beautiful saddle. Your clothing tells us you are a gentleman."

" My name's Key. Francis Scott Key. I'm a lawyer at Frederick, on my way to Annapolis on business."

" I'm afraid your business will have to wait a few days."

Frank lifted himself on his elbow. " Oh, but it can't! " he protested. " I must get to Annapolis by tomorrow night."

She shook her head. " You were badly beaten," she said, " and the blow on your head split it open like a pumpkin. But get a good night's sleep and we shall see how you are in the morning."

When Frank awoke, he moved his arms and legs ex-

perimentally. He winced. It would be very painful to
ride, but he couldn't bear the thought of remaining
where he was when he could be with Mary. He felt himself over carefully. There were no broken bones. His
head was clear, even though it throbbed when he lifted it.

There was a knock at his door.

" Come in," he called.

It was the innkeeper. " My wife sent you some broth,"
he said. " How do you feel this morning? "

" Much better, thank you, due to your kindness. I can
never repay you."

" Think nothing of it. That's our business, helping the
traveler along his way, whatever his need." The little
man was round and jocund. Frank was thankful to have
fallen into his hands.

His host propped the pillows behind his back and set
the bowl of soup before him.

" Ah! This is delicious! " Frank said. He looked about
the room. " I wonder — — My clothes — "

" My wife is trying to clean them a little."

" I was thinking about getting up shortly. I should be
on my way."

The little man looked at him and shook his head. " A
powerful rush you're in. Looks like your business could
wait a day or two."

Frank felt like confiding in his benevolent host. He
smiled. " I suppose my law business could, as a matter
of fact, but you see there's a girl."

The innkeeper began to laugh, and his fat jowls shook.
" Now I understand! " he said. " Well, there's no better
medicine. I'll bring your clothes as soon as my wife fin-

ishes with them."

Frank climbed painfully out of bed and paced about the room to limber his stiff muscles. When he saw his clothes, he shook his head. They were a sorry mess, even after the good woman had done her best with them. She had used her needle to repair the worst of the rents, but the result reminded Frank of a beggar's costume. He laughed ruefully as he struggled into his coat. Am I going to call on Polly this way? he wondered. Too bad Uncle Philip was no longer in Annapolis, but perhaps Roger Taney or Dan Murray could let him have some clothes.

The little innkeeper was there to help him down the stairs.

" How did I get up here last night? " Frank asked.

" We carried you."

Before he left he insisted that the innkeeper give him a complete bill, including an itemized statement of his wife's services in nursing him and repairing his clothes. " I'll be back within the week," he said, " and I assure you you'll get your money. I have good friends in Annapolis."

" I'm not worried about my money. It's you I'm worried about, riding all day."

" Luckily I've the short end of my journey ahead of me."

It was slower going than Frank had anticipated. Much of the time he had to hold his horse to a walk, and the miles seemed interminable. Only the thought of seeing Polly at the end of the journey kept him going. It was well after dark by the time he reached the outskirts of the city.

What should he do? Go to Taney's lodgings? Go to an inn? He kept asking himself these questions, but Comet plodded steadily toward the Lloyds', and he let him go.

I have no business arriving like this, he thought. If there are guests, Polly will never forgive me. But he continued to ride toward her door.

Comet's hoofs on the paved court caused doors to fly open and heads to peer out. Then there were sharp exclamations, and black folks and white poured forth. Loving black hands helped Frank from his horse; then Polly was beside him. " O Frank! Frank! What happened to you? "

Frank saw that she was crying. He smiled to reassure her. " Bandits attacked me last night on the road, but that was last night. Tonight I'm here. That's all that matters."

Colonel Lloyd met them on the veranda.

" My apologies, Sir, for coming to your door like this," Frank said.

But Colonel Lloyd was as kind as the others. Before Frank knew what was happening, they had him in bed and were feeding him a hot supper. He stayed in bed all the next day and was content the day after to sit about the house like an invalid, a shawl over his knees, and be pampered by Polly.

" You're all so good to me, I'll never want to leave," he said. " But I'll have to," he added sadly, his eyes following Polly's every move. It was late afternoon, and the others had left them alone in the parlor. There was a crackling fire in the fireplace which made a soft circle of light that the twilight could not blot out, but the corners of the room were shadowed. Polly pulled up a stool and sat beside him. For a few minutes they gazed into the fire. Then Frank turned his eyes on the bright head at his knee. He reached out and touched her hair.

She made no move, only raised her eyes to look at him. She was smiling. " O Frank," she said, " I'm so thankful you're here. Why, they might have killed you! "

" And you would have cared, Polly? "

Sudden tears flooded her eyes.

" Don't feel badly. They didn't kill me, and with the fine care I'm getting I'll be as good as new in a day or so. But then I'll have to leave you again. Polly, I know you're only sixteen, but — "

" I'll be seventeen soon."

" Bless you. Do you mean — Polly, do you mean that you'll marry me when you're seventeen? "

" Of course you'd have to ask Papa," she said demurely.

" Polly! Polly darling! " He reached down and took her tenderly in his arms. The firelight suffused them in a rosy glow, and Frank felt an answering glow in his heart.

13

ON THE POTOMAC

The Lloyd-Key wedding was the most fashionable of the season. All Annapolis agreed on that. It was on a cold day in January that guests thronged the Lloyd mansion, not only from Annapolis, but from Frederick, from Washington, and from Baltimore as well. But as his lovely, fair-haired bride came down the marble staircase into the white-paneled drawing room, Frank was oblivious to the guests. He saw only his Polly, in white satin and lace, smiling her little inscrutable smile, coming regally to meet him. There was a lump in his throat. Life could be no better to a man than this. He stood straight and proud in his plum-colored coat and white stock and smiled a lifelong welcome to the seventeen-year-old girl who in a few moments would be his wife. The day he had waited for so long had come.

The rest of the day was a blur to Frank — the reception, the gifts, the guests. But at last he and Polly were in the carriage on the way to Frederick.

"I wish I didn't have to take you to Frederick," he said. "It hasn't much to offer an Annapolis girl."

"I didn't have to come. Remember you said if I'd

rather wait and be married next summer, we'd go straight to Washington. I'm glad I decided not to wait."

"So am I," he said, smiling at her and reaching for her hand. "But I keep thinking I should warn you. I don't suppose there are more than five hundred houses in Frederick. The people are hard-working, middle-class men and women with no time for frivolities. You'll miss the parties and the theater — "

Polly interrupted him. " I'll have you, won't I? Don't you think I can enjoy a quiet evening before the fire with my husband? "

Frank laughed. " *A* quiet evening, yes, but I don't know about month after month of them."

The evening was cold and gray when they drove down an unpretentious street in Frederick and stopped before a little brick house which Frank had rented.

" It isn't much, Polly, but it won't be for long. It's the best I could find."

" Frank, will you quit apologizing? " Polly said. " It's a sweet little house."

The door opened. " Welcome, Massa Key! Welcome, Mis' Key! " It was Aunt Sue from Terra Rubra, sent to help Polly.

A blazing fire on the hearth greeted them, and the fragrance of baking ham was wafted from the kitchen.

" How nice! " Polly said, standing before the fire to warm her hands.

" You're tired, Polly," Frank said, " from all that bouncing and jouncing. Here, let me take your things."

Polly laughed. " My poet! " she said. " He puts the simplest sentence into rhyme! "

Frank was very busy at the office in the days that followed. There was plenty of law business and to spare, now that there were eighty grist mills working in Frederick, besides iron furnaces, glassworks, paper mills, and distilleries. There was lots of westward expansion too, for a new state of Ohio had been added to the Union, and President Jefferson had just bought a large tract of land, called the Louisiana Territory, to add to the Union's possessions. Conestoga wagons and stagecoaches often stopped in Frederick on their way west.

"You know what I'm going to do?" Frank said to Polly one night. "I'm going to write Taney and suggest that he come to Frederick and put out his shingle. He says there are too many lawyers in Annapolis and Baltimore already. I know he isn't making a decent living in Annapolis. If he were, he would marry Ann."

Polly smiled. "Matchmaker!" she chided him.

"You can't blame me, can you?" he said. "I want my sister and my best friend to be as happy as I am."

Taney responded to Frank's suggestion. He came to Frederick for a visit and decided to stay. From then on there were gay Sundays at Terra Rubra for the four young people, and many pleasant evenings in the little Key house in Frederick.

Before they knew it the winter was over and spring had come, then summer. It was time for Frank and Polly to move to Washington. They left arrangements to Uncle Philip, who secured a house for them in Georgetown, across the river from the Capital. "It's more fitting for your bride," he wrote, "than anything in Washington. It's a beautiful old house overlooking the Potomac." There was more about the house; then Uncle Philip went into a long description of his own estate, "Woodley," which he had nurtured from nothing into a place of beauty.

Frank and Polly said good-by to Frederick and Terra

Rubra and took the stagecoach to Washington. They stopped over in Annapolis to see Polly's family, then were on their way again.

" It seems strange to think we shan't have Taney dropping in evenings," Frank said.

"Yes," Polly said, " yet I think Frederick is the place for him."

"So do I," Frank agreed. "He's building up a fine practice. I wish he and Ann would get married."

"They will," Polly laughed.

"Polly," Frank said suddenly, " what if law isn't the right profession for me? "

She looked at him earnestly from under the brim of her hat. "You were doing every bit as well in Frederick as Roger Taney."

"Yes, and with Uncle Philip taking me on in Washington, things are likely to go well for me there. It isn't lack of success I'm thinking about — " He left the sentence in mid-air.

After a moment Polly said softly, " What is it you're thinking about, Frank? "

" It's hard to put into words, but I've always had a feeling that I wanted to be of some real service to my fellow men, to my country — "

" I should think you could do that in law, especially practicing in the Capital."

" That's what Taney said when I tried to explain to him how I felt. I don't know what it is. It's as if there is a deeper need within me that solving people's problems through a court of law doesn't satisfy."

" Perhaps it's your poetry."

Frank looked at her in surprise. " I'd never thought of that," he said. " Of course I like to write it, but I'd never thought of it as anything but fun. Not as a career, certainly. No, I can't see myself supporting you on poetry, Polly! " he laughed.

" But perhaps you need to take it more seriously than you do."

" I doubt that I've the ability. I think I'm more of a rhymester than a poet."

" I don't know, Frank. If you were stirred to write about something great enough, something that seemed very important to you — "

" You're the most important thing in the world to me, and while you've inspired me to write reams of verses, I doubt that there's a poem among them."

They were entering the City of Washington, and they dropped their conversation to exclaim over what they saw.

" I wonder what that building is? " Polly said.

Frank shook his head. " I don't know," he said. " Look at the dust. I remember a friend of Uncle Philip's saying you always found Washington in either a foot of mud or a foot of dust. We've found it in a foot of dust."

Polly sneezed.

" Keep your veil over your face," Frank said.

" It would take more than a veil to keep this dust out," she said, sneezing again.

" It looks pretty bleak, doesn't it? " Frank said, peering in all directions.

" Holes in the ground. Half-raised buildings. I'm afraid our Capital couldn't be called a thing of beauty."

" Far from it." Frank shook his head. He felt much as
he had when he first saw St. John's.

But Georgetown was different. In fact, things looked
different the minute they saw the Potomac. " Oh, it's
beautiful! " Polly exclaimed. " And to think we're to
have a house overlooking it! "

" It's a ribbon of silver," Frank said musingly.

At last they drew up before their house. For a moment
they sat staring at it in silence.

" I don't know as I'd call it beautiful," Frank said at
last. " It's so *narrow*."

Polly laughed. " Come on. Let's go in and explore."

There were two nice-sized rooms on the main floor,
plus an entrance hall with stairways going up and down.
" We'll use one of these rooms for the drawing room,"
Polly said, " and the other for our private sitting room.
They're nice rooms, Frank. Now which shall we do: go
up or down? "

" Let's go down first."

On the floor below they discovered a kitchen and din-
ing room and a conservatory extending toward the river.
" I suppose we'll get used to eating in the basement,"
Frank laughed.

" It isn't exactly the basement," Polly argued. " The
house is just built on two levels. Besides, the view will
make up for everything."

Frank smiled at her. " Shall we go see the upstairs
now? "

They went back to the main floor and up another
flight of stairs. On this level they found two large bedrooms. " Oh, these are lovely rooms! " Polly exclaimed.

"There's still another floor," Frank said, indicating a stairway going up.

"Oh, what fun!" Polly cried. "This is just like a storybook, and we're the hero and heroine, going exploring." She reached for his hand and they went on up to the four small attic bedrooms, hand in hand.

Frank smiled at her childlike happiness. He was excited himself, discovering what their home was like. It would be exciting too, discovering what it was like to practice law in the Capital of one's country.

14

INTRODUCTIONS

Frank! " Polly cried one night. " Guess what? "

" You've discovered a new posy in the conservatory."

Polly laughed. " Come with me this instant and see." But she did not lead him to the conservatory. She led him to her tall secretary in the sitting room, picked up a square white envelope, and handed it to him without a word.

Frank opened it and whistled. " Mr. and Mrs. Philip Barton Key request your presence at a reception in honor of President and Mrs. Jefferson," he read aloud.

Polly's eyes were shining. " I thought you'd be pleased," she said.

" You don't know *how* pleased, Polly. I've always admired Mr. Jefferson. Now to think that I'm going to meet him! "

" And when we've been here only such a little while! "

Frank smiled. " It's nice having an Uncle Philip."

" He's seeing that we meet just everybody, isn't he? " Polly beamed. " I'm going to wear my new blue dress."

" Yes, this is the occasion for it, Polly. I think, since

Washington's death, Jefferson is the greatest man in America," he mused.

" Don't forget Alexander Hamilton! " Polly teased.

" If Taney were here, he wouldn't let me forget. But he couldn't convince me that Hamilton is Jefferson's equal, nor that Hamilton is right in his thinking."

" I've known you quite a while now," Polly said, smiling up at him, " but it still surprises me to see how you champion the common man when you were born an aristocrat."

" I don't know just what an aristocrat is," Frank said, " but I don't think I am one."

Polly laughed. " Wealth, breeding, education. They're what make an aristocrat, and you were born to them. Yet it's the man without them that you champion."

" Because I think he's just as important in a democracy as I or any other man who, by an accident of birth, has greater opportunities."

There was a soft footfall outside the door. " Dinnah is se'ved, Mis' Key."

" Thank you, Thomas." Polly took Frank's arm, and they started downstairs. " I'm sure that when President Jefferson meets my handsome, aristocratic husband," she said, " he will be as impressed as I am with his simplicity."

Frank laughed. " The lady is calling me a simpleton! "

Polly squeezed his arm. " You know better than that."

The night of the reception, Frank dressed as carefully as Polly. He was most eager to meet Thomas Jefferson.

When Polly finally turned from her mirror in her ice-blue satin frock, Frank was still adjusting his stock.

" Tut! Tut! " she said. " I'll warrant you never dressed with such pains when you were courting Mary Lloyd."

Frank laughed. "You don't need to start being jealous of the President of the United States." Then he saw her, and he caught his breath. " Polly! You're the most beautiful thing I ever saw. You look like a snowflake with a golden halo."

" You're such a goose," Polly laughed softly. " But you do say the loveliest things. My poet, I love you very much."

Frank let out his breath and shook his head. " I'm the luckiest man alive," he said.

When they were announced at the door of the drawing room at Woodley, soft music and the pleasant babble of well-modulated voices met their ears. Frank read the delight in his Uncle Philip's eyes as he saw Polly. No one was more appreciative of a pretty woman than Uncle Philip. Aunt Kate looked very lovely herself, Frank thought, smiling at the regal lady in dark-red brocade at his uncle's side.

" President Jefferson, Mrs. Jefferson, may I have the pleasure of presenting my nephew and his wife, Mr. and Mrs. Francis Scott Key, recently of Annapolis and Frederick, now of Georgetown and Washington."

The President's eyes were warm. Frank bowed low. " It is my very great honor, Sir — "

" Thank you," the President said simply.

Frank was in a daze as he followed Polly about among the other guests. Those heavy brows! he thought. That wide forehead. The generous mouth. Jefferson is a man worthy to be President of our country. He's intelligent and honest and farsighted. It's all there in his face.

His uncle touched his arm. " Come with me," he said. " I want you to have an opportunity to get closer to your idol, so that you won't have to worship from afar."

Frank smiled. He would like nothing better than to get closer to his idol.

" Here we are," Uncle Philip said, leading him to a corner where the President was sitting among giant potted

plants which had been imported to give the effect of a
summer garden. " Mr. President, my nephew is one of
your ardent admirers. I believe he's the most rabid Democrat in the Capital."

" Not rabid," Frank defended himself. " Just sincere."

President Jefferson smiled. " Won't you sit down? I
understand you have joined your uncle's law firm."

" Yes," Frank said. " Since I was fourteen it's been
Uncle Philip's hope to have me practice with him one
day. I don't know why." He spread his hands.

" Philip Key is a keen judge of men," the President
said, studying Frank closely. " I'm sure he considers you
a valuable addition to the law in Washington. We need
the best lawyers in the country here, like your uncle. I'm
glad you've come to the Capital to join him."

" Having you say that means more than you will ever
know, Mr. President. When I was a boy, I met George
Washington when he visited my father's home in Frederick County. That was the greatest day of my life until
today, which I consider of equal importance."

" You pay me a very high compliment," the President
said.

On the way home in the carriage, Frank could talk of
nothing but the President.

" I don't believe you knew anyone else was there,"
Polly chided him.

" I didn't," Frank admitted. " I wonder why Vice-
President Aaron Burr wasn't there," he added. " I guess
feeling isn't too good between him and the President,
at least on Burr's part."

" You mean because of the election? "

" Yes, Burr was bitter at not getting the Presidency."

" He really had it, just as much as Jefferson, didn't he? "

Frank nodded. " They had an equal number of electoral votes, so it was up to the House of Representatives to decide. Taney's friend Alexander Hamilton was really the one that defeated Burr."

" You should at least give him credit for that! "

" Indeed I do. Though I've never met Burr, I can't believe he could hold a candle to Thomas Jefferson."

But Frank was to meet Aaron Burr before his first winter in the Capital was over. He and Polly were invited to Woodley for dinner with the family one evening. After dinner, Polly was in the upstairs sitting room with the ladies, Frank in the study with his uncle, when a servant came to announce that Mr. Key had a caller, Vice-President Aaron Burr.

A smile flicked over Uncle Philip's face. " I want you to meet him, Frank," he said. " Bring the gentleman in here, George."

Frank stood with his uncle, and eagerly watched the door.

" I wonder what he wants," Uncle Philip said under his breath.

The man whom George brought into the room was short of stature, but his carriage indicated that he tried desperately to make himself look taller. He looks as if he's about to tip over backward, Frank thought.

" Mr. Vice-President," Uncle Philip said, stepping forward and bowing with deference over the visitor's hand.

He likes the deference, Frank thought, but not being called Vice-President.

" This is my nephew, Francis Scott Key, my new law partner," Uncle Philip introduced him.

On the instant, Frank decided to use Burr's name instead of his title. " Mr. Burr," he said.

The eyes of the little man bored intently into his as if to let him know he saw his strategy plainly. Then he ignored the younger Mr. Key as if he had not been in the room.

Frank sat back and listened. He did not mind being treated as if he were nonexistent. It gave him a better opportunity to study this man. He'd heard many tales about him. Now he was glad of his opportunity to make his own judgments.

Mr. Burr had come about a point of law. He could have sent a messenger, Frank thought, or come to the office. His business was of no great consequence or immediate concern. He wanted to come here. He likes Uncle Philip's regal establishment. Or is it that he wants to boast of having been here? I believe that's it.

After a time, the guest rose to go.

" I'm glad to have had an opportunity to meet you, Mr. Burr," Frank said.

" Thank you." They were exactly the words President Jefferson had used when Frank expressed gratitude at meeting him. But how different they sounded! Aaron Burr's tone plainly said, " You *should* be gratified to meet me, young man." Frank had to bite back a smile.

" Well, what did you think of him? " Uncle Philip

asked, coming back into the room.

" A lot of things," Frank said, letting the smile out, now that the guest was gone.

Uncle Philip nodded. " He's clever as a fox," he said.

" And as dangerous, I'd warrant," Frank added.

" Along with your other talents, I believe you've the ability to judge men," his uncle said. " Let's hear what else you decided about him."

" I think he's an arrogant and bitter fool," Frank said.

His uncle looked at him in some surprise. As far as he could remember, he'd never heard Frank speak vehemently against anyone before.

" I think he's letting his defeat eat at his vitals like a cankerworm. Of course, he's clever, as sharp as a honed razor. But I think he'd use his cleverness to slit a man's throat as soon as not. In short, I wouldn't trust him from here to where you're standing."

15

POLITICS

Let's take a walk along the river," Polly said to Frank one evening after dinner. "It can't be good for you to stick your nose into those old lawbooks the minute you finish eating."

Frank wrinkled his nose at her. "And it isn't good for you to have such a dull husband. Get your bonnet and let's go."

"I don't want a bonnet; it's such a lovely evening."

Arm in arm they went out through the conservatory and strolled toward the river.

"You didn't know I saw Uncle Philip in town today, did you?" Polly asked.

"Oh, but I did. He told me he had lunch with you, and I turned green with envy." Frank's eyes smiled on her.

"I met him as I was coming out of the doctor's office, and he insisted that I lunch with him."

"All very well except that I should have been with him."

"That was what I said, but he said you were very busy working on a poor widow's case that you wouldn't get a cent out of."

Frank eyed her sidewise.

" I learned quite a bit about my husband that I didn't know before," she said mischievously.

" Like my working for nothing? Well, Uncle Philip and I get big enough fees from our well-to-do clients to make up for it. You don't mind, do you, as long as I make enough to support you ' in the style to which you've been accustomed,' as Uncle Philip would say? "

" I was very proud when he told me you did some of your best work for Negroes and poor people who couldn't pay."

" Well, they need help."

" You don't need to defend yourself to me, Frank. I think everything you do is perfect."

" That's because you're a perfect wife."

Polly looked up at him seriously. " Don't you feel satisfied now with the law? "

He looked into her solemn, upturned face, and took her chin gently in his hand. " Don't worry about me," he said. " The law's all right. If I should decide to meddle in politics a little, I'll do it on the side."

" Then you are still thinking about politics? "

Frank laughed. " Everyone in the Capital thinks about politics. It's in the wind. You can't escape it."

" Has the President suggested something? " Polly was proud that Frank had become a friend of President Jefferson and from time to time was called in for conferences with him and his advisers.

" Nothing definite," Frank said. Then he asked: " Did Uncle Philip tell you about **Judge Chase** being impeached? "

" Yes, and I think it's a shame. The poor old man! "

" Of course he does have a beastly temper. Uncle Philip
will be one of the counsel to defend him, so I'll get to
listen in on the trial."

Frank's emotions were mixed as he walked to the Senate Chambers the opening day of Judge Chase's trial, carrying an armload of lawbooks for his uncle. Judge Samuel Chase, who had built the beautiful Lloyd mansion in
which Polly had grown up; the Signer of the Declaration
of Independence; the judge whom Frank had called
" Old Bacon Face " in a schoolboy poem; the Justice
whom George Washington had appointed to the Supreme Court. Frank took his seat beside his uncle feeling
that his party was desecrating something venerable, ac-
cusing the old judge of misconduct in office.

Aaron Burr, as Vice-President, was in charge of the
trial. He looked very sleek and smug, Frank thought,
strutting about. I may as well admit I don't like the man,
he said to himself.

There was a bustle of interest among the Senators and
Frank looked up to see Judge Chase being conducted to
the Chambers. He caught his breath. The Judge was an
old man now. His hair was white. The red face that had
inspired the boys to call him " Bacon Face " had grown
pouchy and splotched. Rolls of fat fell from it in double
and triple chins. His six-foot frame sagged with fat. He
leaned heavily on a cane. Gout, Frank thought. A feeling
verging on revulsion came over him. Yet it was for his
mind that George Washington appointed the man to the
Bench, he reminded himself.

His attention turned from the Judge to the Vice-Presi-

dent. There seemed to be some point of contention between him and the Judge's chief counsel. Then Frank
caught a few words and understood. The counsel was
arguing that the Judge should be seated. Burr would have
him stand. Burr stared contemptuously at the old Judge.

Finally, in a sneering tone that could be heard throughout the Chambers, he said, " If the accused is so old and decrepit that he can't stand, he may be seated."

The hair stood up on the back of Frank's neck. The words had been a deliberate insult. Why did the man want to make himself so hatefully disagreeable?

The trial got under way. John Randolph, whom Frank had met casually at Woodley, was in charge of the prosecution. Frank studied him with interest. He was a tall, rangy Virginian with a handsome head, a high-pitched voice, and more than an ordinary flair for oratory. Was he going to be a second Patrick Henry? He presented his charges and began calling his witnesses.

At first the political play and byplay involved in the case intrigued Frank, but as the days went by and the trial dragged endlessly on, his interest turned to disgust.

One afternoon, when the defense was presenting its case, his Uncle Philip rose to speak. Before he had taken two steps, a sharp voice cut through the Chambers. " Mr. Key! You cannot be permitted to appear as counsel in that loose cloak! " It was Aaron Burr. Frank flushed in anger and sprang to his feet. He wanted to clutch Aaron Burr's arrogant throat in his long fingers. In two strides he was at his uncle's side.

Uncle Philip was smiling blandly, unperturbed. " Well, then," he said, " if you object to my coat, Mr. Chairman, permit me to exchange it for my nephew's. I'm sure his is in the proper style to please you, and on me it should not be loose! "

A ripple of laughter rose from the Senate floor. Frank admired his uncle's poise, but he himself was still angry.

His lips did not smile as he removed his coat and helped his uncle into it.

" Quite tight enough, I'm sure," his uncle said, turning to face the Chamber and pulling the coat taut across his stomach.

Another wave of laughter came from the Senators. Frank turned and strode back to his place, his uncle's coat over his arm. He felt as irritable as a small boy who had been stopped at the outset of a good fight. What's the matter with me? he thought. Am I upset out of all proportion to the annoyance? Of course, he was worried about Polly: her baby was due any day now. But it seemed that ever since this trial had begun, his nerves had been jagged.

Polly chided him gently at home that evening. They were in the sitting room, Polly knitting and Frank poring over a lawbook. " I'll be glad when Judge Chase's trial is over," she said. " You haven't been yourself since the day it began."

Frank looked up in surprise. " Polly! " he cried. " Have I been irritable at home? Darling, you know I haven't meant to be." He dropped his book on the floor and strode across the room to her, his brows knit in concern.

Polly laid down her knitting and indicated the stool at her feet. " Sit down here," she said. " No, you haven't been irritable to me, Frank. I think you're the most considerate husband any girl ever had. It's just that I can tell you're upset. What is it that's bothering you so? Can't you tell me? "

Frank sighed. " I don't like to bother you," he said.

" It only bothers me to know that you're unhappy. It

will never bother me to have you tell me your troubles.
A good marriage must be a complete sharing, Frank, of
unhappiness as well as happiness. Tell me."

He leaned his head against her knee. " It's all so bitter," he said. " I can't bear it."

Polly nodded. Her eyes were understanding.

" The hurling of invective! The hatred! I can't stand
it, Polly. At the end of a day of it, I feel raw. It's as if
everyone were hurling sharp knives, and while the weap-
ons aren't aimed at me, each one cuts as it flies by. Politics! Was I ever fool enough to think I wanted to enter
politics? To think that I might do some good for my
country that way? This party strife! The anger, the
jealousy, the pettiness! I want none of it."

" No, I can see it's not for you," Polly said gently.
" You have too much of your father's gentle soul, too
much of the peace of Terra Rubra — "

It was a relief to know that Polly understood. Unbur-
dening himself of the distress with which this political
tug of war had filled him acted like a panacea. He could
go back to the trial now and be less a part of it. He knew
and Polly knew that he would never be a party to the
cruelty and ruthlessness of politics. If he didn't have to,
he wouldn't even be a spectator in the arena again.

It was the last day of the trial. John Randolph had
summed up the case for the prosecution in his high-flown
oratory. He had ended by pointing a finger at the impres-
sive array of Federalists acting as counsel for the defense.
" Perhaps Judge Chase thought to impress the Senate by
the number and fame of his counsel, but I'm sure the
Senate is not impressed. They are impressed by evidence,

not by names. We leave the decision to them, trusting that in their good judgment they will see that the misdemeanors committed by the defendant make him unfit for the duties of the highest court in the land."

A messenger touched Frank's arm and handed him a note. Without another moment's thought for the trial, Frank jumped up and strode from the Chambers. As he grabbed his hat, he looked again at the note in his hand. It shook before his eyes. A girl! Polly had borne him a daughter!

Late in the afternoon, his uncle stopped by the house on the Potomac. " I had to congratulate the new father! " he said, throwing an arm about Frank in the fatherly way he had assumed when Frank was a boy. " How's Polly? "

" Fine! She's the happiest girl alive. We've named our daughter Elizabeth Phoebe. But the trial! " Frank cried, suddenly remembering. " Is it over? "

" Yes, it's over, thank the Lord, and Judge Chase is still a member of the Supreme Court."

" You mean the Senate didn't remove him? "

" No. Did you think they would? " Uncle Philip laughed. "A lot of faith you had in our case! "

" I didn't mean it that way," Frank said. "It's just that it seems like such a frightful display of venom, such a waste of men's energies and talents. So much hatred was engendered." He shook his head. " And for what? Nothing."

" That's politics, Frank. It isn't always pretty."

" I want none of it," Frank said emphatically.

His uncle twirled his hat. " Oh? " he said. " Well, I

must get on home now. We'll talk about politics some other time. Give my love to Polly."

" Indeed I will."

Frank wondered if Uncle Philip had some political plum in mind for him. Or was he thinking about himself and politics? He had something up his sleeve. Well, if it was a political job for his nephew, he'd as well know at the outset that his nephew wasn't interested. Frank felt a positive revulsion for politics. But as for being a family man, that stirred his heart with pride!

16

THE STAR–SPANGLED FLAG

Within the year Frank learned that it was not for his nephew but for himself that Uncle Philip had political aspirations.

" Frank," he said one day, leaning back in his walnut office chair, " what would you think if I told you I was going to run for Congress? "

" I'd think what I've thought since the day I met you: that you're the most ambitious fellow ever born into the Key family." He studied his uncle's fine head with admiration. The years had only enhanced the distinguished appearance of Philip Barton Key. " And you'll win," he added with a chuckle. " Though you're a Federalist running for office when the Democrats are in power, you'll still win."

" Well, if I didn't think I had a good chance, I wouldn't run," his uncle said shrewdly.

" So what about the law offices of Key and Key? " Frank asked.

" That's up to you. I'll give up practicing, of course, if I'm elected."

It left Frank a good deal to think about in the months to come.

" I think perhaps I'll move my office to the house when Uncle Philip leaves," he said to Polly one night the following year, when his uncle's campaign was in full swing.

She threw up her hands. " Mercy! " she cried. " How could you work with the babies crying? "

Frank smiled. " One reason I'd like to be here," he said, " is so I can tend to the education of the children. If I have my office at home, I can budget my time so that I can give two or three hours each morning to teaching them."

" They don't need a tutor quite yet, dear," Polly said with a smile. Their second daughter, Maria Lloyd, was not yet a month old, and Elizabeth Phoebe not yet two years.

Frank laughed. " I'm planning for the future," he said.

Uncle Philip was elected, as Frank had predicted, and Frank moved his lawbooks across the Potomac and into the room that had been the family sitting room. Polly's desk and the comfortable chairs went to the second floor, where Polly turned one of the large bedrooms into an upstairs sitting room. She moved the nursery to the third floor. " Now you won't be able to hear the babies cry," she told Frank.

" Polly, you're wonderful. How do you put up with me? Whatever my notions, you always fall in with them, no matter how much trouble they cause you."

" Oh, I'll be very glad to have you here to attend to the children's education," she said, laughing up at him.

" The only trouble is, I'll be tempted to neglect my business; I enjoy being with you and the babies so much."

" I have *my* business too," she said, " the house, the

servants, the children. I can't have you interfering with it! " She said it with a smile, but Frank knew she meant it. So he set his office hours and stuck to them. Trying to handle the law practice alone was a big job. He had no more time to interfere with Polly's work than she had time to interfere with his.

" As if I didn't have enough to do, they ask me to write

poems! " he said aloud late one afternoon, when his last
client had gone and he was straightening the papers on
his desk. He had been asked to write a poem for a banquet
heralding the return of the naval officers who had put
down the Barbary pirates to make the Mediterranean
safe for American merchantmen. He sat in the gathering
twilight hoping for an inspiration. The banquet was the
following night. He couldn't put the poem off much
longer. Suddenly, into his mind came the tune he had
first heard in Frederick years before when John Adams
was running for a second term as President. With the
" Adams and Liberty " words, it had made a fine campaign song. But it was the tune — the tune of the old
song " To Anacreon in Heaven " — that had impressed
Frank then, and which he started humming now. " It's
a rousing tune," he said aloud.

He pulled pen and paper toward him and began to
write a poem to the rhythm of the song. The twilight
deepened, and a servant came in to light the lamps.

" You-all's wo'kin' late tonight, Massa Key."

Frank nodded without looking up. Words trailed across
the white sheet before him into lines; lines piled up into
stanzas. He was still writing when dinner was announced.
He picked up the paper and took it with him. He and
Polly were dining alone tonight. He would let her read
what he had written. She was a discerning critic, and she
was always interested in his poetry.

After he had said grace, he handed her the paper. " You
knew I had to write a poem to read at the banquet tomorrow night. I've just scribbled this off. Remember the
tune ' To Anacreon in Heaven ' that they used to sing

the ' Adams and Liberty ' words to? "

Polly nodded.

" It has such a wonderful swing to it," Frank said. " I was trying to use the pattern of it for my poem."

While the soup plates were being removed, Polly began to read. " This has a splendid rhythm," she said, her voice pleased. She read on in silence. After a moment, she looked up at him. " I like this line: ' By the light of the star-spangled flag of our nation.' Star-spangled flag. That's beautiful, Frank. It describes the flag to perfection. How do you do it? "

Frank only smiled at her bright, bowed head.

" That's the best line in it," she said again when she had finished. " ' By the light of the star-spangled flag of our nation.' "

When he read the poem at the banquet, the room rang with applause. But as he walked home under the starlit sky, he felt vaguely despondent. What's the matter with me? he wondered. He had enjoyed an evening of good food and good company and praise for his verses. What more could he ask? Of course, there had been talk of war, which always depressed him. But he had faith in Jefferson. The President's efforts to preserve peace with England and France had been successful so far. What reason was there to believe his success would not continue?

There was no light in the upstairs sitting room when he arrived home, which meant that Polly had gone to bed. He wasn't sleepy, although it was past midnight. He would sit in his office for a while and think.

I wish I were more a man of action, like Uncle Philip, he thought; then perhaps I could get rid of this longing that nags me, this thing inside me that's always unsatisfied, always pushing me toward something. The trouble is, I don't know what the something is. Is Polly right that it's my poetry? Should I give it more serious consideration?

My friends think I'm the luckiest and happiest man alive. I certainly am the luckiest; no man could be happier in his family. I love Polly more every day, and I adore the babies. I have more law business than I can handle; I'm making a splendid living; we have everything we want in a material way. I have wonderful friends. Ann and Taney are married at last. We have glorious summers at Terra Rubra. I have everything, in short, and still I have this feeling of futility and unfulfillment.

He put his head in his hands and began to pray, talking with his Creator as he might have talked to Polly.

" It isn't that I'm ungrateful, God," he said. " I've been thankful for Polly since the day I met her; you know that. And I'm thankful for Uncle Philip's help in launching me in my career. I'm thankful for the opportunities I have to do good in my practice, but they're not enough. I want to make a real contribution to the world. My father set me to thinking I'd have something special to give when I was just a boy. Maybe I really don't have. But if I do, won't you show it to me? I'm more than willing, if I only knew what I could do. Please, God, show me the way. Amen."

After a little, he turned up the light and rummaged in the bottom drawer of his desk until he found a carefully wrapped parcel. It was the flag Ann had made for him when he first left Terra Rubra. He spread it on his desk and smoothed out the folds, and his mind went back to the happy, carefree days when he and Ann were children.

I promised George Washington I would always honor the flag, he thought; that I've done. But I promised myself I'd do something for my country that was worthy of the flag, and that I haven't done. That's what I'm seeking.

His hand caressed the flag, and as it caught the light from the lamp, his throat tightened. How beautiful it is, he thought, with its broad stripes and bright stars! I wonder why it stirs me so deeply? Is it because it, like the Constitution, was " conceived in liberty "?

It was very late. He did not refold the flag, but left it spread over the top of his desk like a map — a map of freedom, he thought, as he rose to go up to bed. He stood looking at it for a long moment before he put out the light. " I hope my children, and their children, and their children's children will always keep it free," he said softly.

17

TREASON

Frank glanced up at the messenger who stood beside his desk. " No answer," he said. " I will come at once." He looked again at the message: " You are wanted immediately at the President's office." This was by no means the first time he had been summoned to a conference with the President, but there was an urgency about this message that alarmed him. Did it mean war? War clouds continued to threaten ominously, but Frank still hoped and prayed that war could be averted.

He grabbed his hat and coat and strode out into the damp December day.

The minute he stepped inside the President's house, he could feel excitement in the air. He half expected the doorman who took his things to say, " It's war, Massa Key! " But he only commented on the weather.

As Frank was admitted to the President's private office, he saw that the President was seated at his desk and that a number of his advisers were already there. The atmosphere was tense.

" It's Aaron Burr again," a man hissed in his ear as he dropped into a chair.

Frank's brows drew together. What had Aaron Burr done now? The scandal of his killing Alexander Hamilton in a duel was still hot on people's lips.

The President peered out from under his shaggy brows. " I believe we're all here," he said. " Most of you have heard the scandalous news that's brought us together. Aaron Burr's turned traitor! Tell the gentlemen what you've learned, Mr. Randolph."

Frank's gaze darted to John Randolph. His long jaw seemed to jut out even farther than usual. His eyes burned in their deep sockets.

" Though we don't quite know what he's about," he said, " we know enough to tell us he's up to no good. He's outfitting barges at Blennerhassett's island in the Ohio River. He's got men and ammunition ready to load on board and push off for the-Lord-knows-where, but obviously with the intent of taking some territory that doesn't belong to him and setting himself up as monarch." Randolph's tone was bitter. " We suspect it's the Louisiana Purchase or some portion of it that he's after."

Frank let out an audible gasp as the words whipped off Randolph's tongue. He had mistrusted Burr from the moment he met him in his uncle's home, yet he hadn't thought him a fool. This sounded like the weird scheme of a twisted, half-crazed mind. Suddenly it came to him that that was what it was. The man had let his bitter jealousy prey upon his mind until he was no longer sane. Frank felt a wave of pity along with one of revulsion, for this man who might have done great good for his country had he made unselfish use of his talents.

" The poor fool," he muttered.

" What steps have been taken to stop him? " someone demanded.

" The President has ordered the Ohio militia out to watch the river," Randolph answered. " The barges haven't put off."

" Where is Burr? " Frank demanded.

" That we don't know," Randolph admitted. " He isn't at the island; neither is Blennerhassett. But it won't be hard to trace them. They have to get orders through to the island."

" Do you know their strength? " Frank asked.

" They have fifteen large barges," Randolph answered, " enough to transport a powerful force of men. We know men are gathering, but we don't know how many are on the island, nor, of course, how many more will come."

" It's fantastic," Frank said.

" Aaron Burr is a dangerous man! " the President barked. " He must be captured at once and brought to trial for treason."

Frank's law-trained mind jumped ahead. What real evidence was there that Burr was contemplating treason? Circumstantial, perhaps. But could his intentions be proved treasonable?

Frank found that he was tremendously excited, and he thought he had never seen the President so worked up over anything before. He didn't actually think, did he, that Aaron Burr would attempt to overthrow the United States Government with his fifteen barges and odd gathering of men? That he would try to take the United States and usurp the President's office?

" I've called you together to plan our course of action," the President said.

" It would seem imperative to alert the Virginia militia," someone said.

Jefferson nodded.

" And to put out a warrant for Burr's and Blennerhassett's arrest," Randolph said, looking at Frank.

Frank said nothing. The whole thing still struck him like some strange fairy tale out of his small daughters' storybooks.

When the conference broke up, he hurried home to tell Polly the story. But it was with no thought that he would have an active part to play in the drama.

Often of an evening Frank's friends dropped in to talk. Frank was popular among the young professional men, and his home was a pleasant place to stop. " You and your friends should have every problem of the world settled by now," Polly laughed one night when a session had lasted past midnight.

" That's the trouble," Frank admitted. " We never settle anything. We just air our views. It was slavery we were off on last night."

But now they could talk of nothing but the strange case of Aaron Burr. One night the excitement ran high.

" They've captured him! " cried a young man, as he was shown into Frank's study.

" No! Where? "

" In Virginia somewhere. I didn't get the details. I just ran into Lane, who'd seen Randolph. All I learned was that he'd been arrested and that Henry Clay will defend him."

" How I'd like to hear that trial! " Frank cried.

In the days that followed, he thought seriously of going to Richmond to attend the Burr trial. Every lawyer he knew was hoping to go. He tried to get his work in shape so he could leave. But just when it began to look as if he could get away, something happened to change his plans.

Two more men were apprehended in the Burr case. One of them Frank knew personally and the other he had heard much about. They had been caught trying to deliver coded letters from Aaron Burr to General Wilkinson in New Orleans. The one whom Frank had met was a doctor by the name of Bollman.

" He's the fellow that tried to help Lafayette escape when Napoleon had him imprisoned! " Frank told Polly excitedly.

" He must like adventure," Polly said.

" No doubt of it," Frank agreed. " But I've a warm place in my heart for the fellow, all the same. Don't forget that my father fought with Lafayette in the Revolution."

Polly nodded.

" Not that that has anything to do with this case." He was silent a few minutes, and Polly watched him, waiting. Then he said, " They sent for me today."

" You mean Dr. Bollman and this other man? "

Frank nodded. " Bollman and Swartwout. They're in custody of the Federal marshal here. The President called me in again too."

He was frowning, and Polly knew something was troubling him. She thought she knew what it was. " Bollman and Swartwout want you to defend them; and of course the President doesn't want you to. Is that it? "

" It amounts to that," Frank admitted. " And although I didn't tell Jefferson so, I think I'm going to take their case."

Polly waited, but when he did not go on, she said, " You think they're innocent? "

" I certainly don't think they're guilty of treason, as Jefferson seems to. That's what they're being held for."

Polly had learned long ago that her husband would stand for the right as he saw it, regardless of what pressures he must stand against, so she wasn't surprised that he was willing to take a stand against Jefferson, though he counted the President his friend.

" They haven't received just treatment," he went on, pacing the floor in his earnestness. " Despite writs of habeas corpus (they're orders from the court, you know, that the prisoners be brought in for hearing), they were brought here *without* a hearing."

" Where were they captured? " Polly asked.

" In New Orleans. That General Wilkinson! He's the one that had them arrested. If the truth were known, I shouldn't be surprised if he's in the plot with Burr up to his neck. He's probably trying to save his own skin by turning State's evidence."

But if Polly thought Frank was excited that night, it was as nothing compared to the state he was in the following night. " The President's trying to block my getting a writ of habeas corpus to bring the prisoners into court here in Washington! " he cried. " He's arguing that Bollman and Swartwout are such a threat to the security of the country that they shouldn't be allowed out of jail. Why, it's ridiculous! He's trying to get Congress to suspend the writ of habeas corpus. That's interfering with justice. They've no right to tamper with the law. It's for the judiciary to determine such matters, not the executive or legislative branch of the Government."

" It sounds as if the President is frightened, Frank."

Frank looked at her in surprise. " I hadn't thought of that," he said. " I just thought he was being stubborn. Maybe you're right. But whatever his reason, he can't be allowed to tamper with justice."

They were interrupted by Thomas. " A gentleman to see you, Massa Key."

" Thank you, Thomas. Show him into my study."

Polly sighed. " Another evening that I spend alone! "

" Poor Polly." Frank stopped to kiss her, then hurried into the study.

" John Randolph! " he exclaimed, surprised and pleased. He had admired the lanky Virginian for a long time, though he didn't always agree with him. On the Burr situation, Randolph had been the President's right-hand man. Probably he was here to persuade him to give up fighting Jefferson over the habeas corpus. Still, he was glad to see him, whatever his errand.

" Sit down. I'm honored to have you call."

" Thank you. You've a pleasant place here."

" It serves us very well."

Frank sat down too, waiting for his guest to broach the subject on which he had come. Randolph crossed and un-crossed his long legs, cleared his throat, and said: " I just wanted you to know that I'm with you on this habeas corpus business."

" You're with me? " Frank's tone showed his surprise.

Randolph smiled wryly. " You're surprised."

" Yes," Frank admitted. " I thought you were hand and glove with the President, and he seems determined to interfere with justice in this case."

" I can't agree with him there," Randolph broke in. " Every man should have his chance at a fair trial. I wanted to tell you that even though the President succeeded in getting the Senate to vote to suspend the writ, I'm sure I can prevent the same thing from happening in the House."

Frank jumped up and extended his hand. " Mr. Randolph! " he exclaimed. " That's most kind of you."

" It's just that I think such a step would be unnecessary and tyrannical."

When the time came, John Randolph was successful in the House, as Frank had felt sure he would be. He was a convincing speaker, and he made his colleagues see that in a free country no man's right to trial should rightfully be denied.

On the day of the preliminary hearing for Bollman and Swartwout, Frank dressed with care. He wasn't nervous. He had his case well in hand, his pleading written with care. He was fighting for what he believed to be right, so he had no fears. While his clients were adventurers, he was convinced that they hadn't known what was in the letter they were carrying for Burr, and had had no part in his strange plans, whatever they were.

" You're very handsome, and you're very nice," Polly said, kissing him good-by. " And if you don't win, it won't be your fault."

" Take good care of my son while I'm gone," Frank

said. Polly had borne him a son the past year, and he was extremely proud of him.

" What about your daughters? " Polly asked, pretending to pout.

" Being pretty like their mother, they'll always have someone to take care of them."

Frank left home in high spirits. When he reached the courtroom, it was crowded. The House had adjourned to hear the trial, and there were many Senators present. " They'll have difficulty getting a quorum in the Senate today," he said to his colleagues, Lee and Harper.

Frank pleaded eloquently. Though he was only twenty-eight years old, he'd had much experience in his few years of practice, and he was a born speaker. Just as words flowed easily from his pen when he was writing a poem, so they flowed easily from his lips when he was pleading a case.

There were many men in the courtroom who, though they knew him personally, had never heard him plead a case before.

" He's certainly an original pleader! " one Senator exclaimed.

" A real orator. He has the voice, the enunciation — "

" And enough personal charm to win any jury."

But Frank did not succeed in winning the judges on the Federal court. They had all been appointed to their jobs by Jefferson. They all knew where his sympathies lay. They decided against Frank's clients and sent them back to prison.

However, Frank was not discouraged. " There's still the Supreme Court," he reminded his colleagues. And so the case went to the Supreme Court. There the trial dragged on and on, into February, through February.

" Every place I go," Polly told Frank, " I hear praises of that brilliant young lawyer named Key."

" He isn't brilliant," Frank said. " He just has a couple of colorful clients and a sensational case."

" At any rate, he's certainly building a reputation! "

At long last, the case came to a close, the Supreme Court handed down its decision, and this time Frank had won. He listened intently as the Chief Justice read the majority opinion: " The testimony did not furnish probable cause for supposing that Samuel Swartwout has levied war against the United States." The same opinion was read for Dr. Bollman.

Frank took a long breath and began gathering up his papers. It had been a long, hard case, but he had enjoyed it. Right had won out, even in the face of Presidential opposition. That was the way democracy should work. For the moment he was content.

18

WAR

I may have missed a good trial at Richmond, but I had a good one in Washington," Frank said to Polly that night. He was stretched out in his favorite easy chair in the upstairs sitting room. It was a relief to relax at last, the pressure of the long trial lifted.

" Henry Clay must be almost as good a lawyer as Francis Scott Key," Polly teased, " to get Aaron Burr acquitted."

" I doubted from the first that Burr could be convicted. But, despite his acquittal, his political opportunities are forever ruined."

" I wonder what he'll do."

" Go to Europe, I've heard."

" Did the President ever show you the letter Lafayette wrote him about Dr. Bollman? "

Frank chuckled. " No, I'm no longer in the President's favor. But Randolph told me what was in the letter. Lafayette begged the President to free Bollman. He said Bollman's brave trip to Olmutz in his behalf should offset his indiscreet trip to New Orleans with a letter for Wilkinson."

" And General Wilkinson did just what you said he'd do, didn't he? Testified against Burr to save himself."

Frank nodded. " I believe he's the real culprit, probably in the employ of Spain. Well, the truth will out. I think we'll still see him court-martialed."

" What strange things come out of a trial! " Polly mused. " You've made a new friend in Randolph and lost an old one in Jefferson."

Frank smiled. " John Randolph interests me tremendously though we often disagree. As for Jefferson, he won't be in Washington much longer."

" Who do you think will be the new President? "

" The way the wind's blowing, it looks like James Madison."

" And you don't approve? " Polly asked, catching the hint of displeasure in his tone.

" I can't be enthusiastic. He's a fine scholar, but I doubt that he has the qualities to make a good executive."

Frank's prophecy was borne out. James Madison won the election, and in 1809 was inaugurated as President of the United States. From the first it seemed obvious to Frank that he would be inveigled into war. He was not a strong enough leader to stand out against the warmongers.

The question of war was one thing about which Frank and John Randolph were in absolute accord. Neither could see any good in a war with England. Whenever Frank could, he attended the Congressional debates on the subject. He was tremendously excited the afternoon John Randolph spoke. " He's making one of the greatest speeches I've ever heard! " he whispered to the man sitting next to him in the gallery, as Randolph pleaded passionately against a declaration of war. When Randolph sat down, Frank jumped to his feet to applaud. Looking over the balcony railing into the House Chamber below, he saw to his disappointment that the only Congressmen applauding were the Federalists. That meant but one thing: The Democratic party, of which he and Randolph were members, the party in control, was in favor of war. He trudged home, dejected.

He was not surprised when Randolph appeared at his house that night.

" You should have stayed to hear Henry Clay's reply to my speech," his visitor said dryly.

" I know all that Henry Clay has to say," Frank replied. " I'd venture he said that the blocking of our ports and harbors by England is as serious as invasion of our shores."

" He did."

" Mark my word, Randolph, what Madison and his advisers have in mind is an invasion of Canada. And don't tell me that will be for anybody's good. Those poor, innocent Canadians! I won't fight them. Madison thinks he'd get a little glory out of it. Well, for my part, I say it would be ignominy! "

" The sad thing is that it's going to come, and neither you nor I have the power to stop it."

On a bright day in June, 1812, Frank came out of court to be met by the frenzied cries of newsboys: " Congress declares war! U.S. at war with England! "

His jaw set. " Bring me a paper, boy," he called. The paper shook in his hands as he held it before his eyes.

" Senate votes 19 to 13 for declaration of war against England." His gaze ran on down the column. The House had voted 79 to 49 for war. Philip Barton Key had voted against it. John Randolph had voted against it. But there hadn't been enough Philip Barton Keys and John Randolphs.

Even Polly and the five children that now made up Frank's happy family couldn't dispel his gloom that evening.

The next day he had a case in the little village of Upper Marlboro, fifteen miles away. It was a beautiful June day, in direct contrast to his own black mood, which he had not been able to throw off. He took care of his business and then decided to go spend an hour with his elderly friend, Dr. Beanes. He had met the doctor through a mutual friend, a Mr. West, who was often a member of the groups that sat before Frank's fire discussing politics and religion. The aging doctor interested Frank. On their first meeting they had discovered that they were distantly related, and they always made a joke of this. Dr. Beanes was a Federalist, so the two often disagreed, but on the war, Frank knew, they would be in perfect accord.

" Well, well! This is a surprise! And one that does my old heart good," Dr. Beanes exclaimed when Frank was shown into the pleasant summer garden behind the house, where his host was enjoying a siesta. " Sit down and rest a bit; then you must take a look at my roses. How are Mrs. Key and all the little Keys? "

Frank smiled at the doctor's pleasantry and stretched himself out on a lounge chair. " They're all well, thank you. Polly's busy keeping the bugs off her roses, so they'll be as fine as yours. She sent her regards, in case I should see you."

" Return my greetings to a very beautiful lady, who grows very beautiful roses, though I won't admit they equal mine."

The fragrance of the roses came pleasantly to Frank's nostrils on the soft summer breeze. The garden was a refuge of peace and contentment. This was the way life should be. Why must men tear it to bits with wars?

" This is heaven," he said, " after Washington."

" Everyone's in a stew over the declaration of war, I suppose."

Frank nodded. " My friends the Democrats seem to think they've won a great victory. For my part, I think they've got themselves into a fine mess."

The doctor laughed. " You'd better join the Federalists," he said. " They're not war-minded."

" What you really mean is, they're pro-British."

" I wouldn't go so far as to say that," the doctor demurred.

" Anyway, we're into it," Frank said. " Now what do we do? "

The doctor shook his head. " I suppose you'll be enlisting."

" Not to invade Canada, I won't. And you mark my word, that's what they're going to do. If it comes to defending our own shores, of course I'll fight for my country. But it hasn't come to that yet."

" It likely will, now that they've got us into it."

Their conversation was interrupted by the appearance of a servant. " The three aldermans am heah, Doctah."

" Already? " the doctor said in surprise, pulling out his big gold watch. " I'm sorry to have to cut our visit short, but I have a meeting with the three aldermen about improving our village square."

Frank rose. " That's quite all right," he said. " I know you're busy with civic affairs."

" They depend on me," the doctor said, indicating the town with a sweeping gesture. He rose and extended his hand. " Stop by again, the next time you come this way. And don't forget to remember me to your lovely wife."

Frank hadn't inspected the doctor's roses, but Polly had roses he could enjoy. What disappointed him about the interruption of his visit was the fact that he hadn't had enough time to talk to the doctor about the war. He supposed he'd been hoping that the doctor would some-how raise his spirits — perhaps assure him that the war would not be of long duration or great importance. But he left the house feeling as depressed as when he had ar-rived.

Dr. Beanes was a regular " town father," he thought, as he mounted his horse. He was a brilliant man of medi-cine, yet he chose to remain a country doctor in this little town which paid him great honor and respect. He was a man of considerable wealth, the owner of the town's grist mill and a number of nearby farms. He entertained lavishly in his beautiful home. He directed every civic enterprise. The townspeople depended on him to make decisions. All this, to the doctor, must add up to satis-faction in living, for he seemed highly content.

Frank sighed as he turned his horse's head toward home. For, though outwardly he seemed to have all life's satisfactions, he did not know content.

19

SOLDIERING

Frank's discontent grew in the months that followed. He missed his friend, John Randolph, who had failed of re-election to Congress and had left Washington. His law practice had fallen off alarmingly since the declaration of war. He didn't have enough to keep his mind occupied, even though he now spent several hours a day teaching his children. And, finally, he couldn't afford to continue practicing law if he couldn't make a living at it.

While he was debating what he should do, the war's turn of events decided things for him. The invasion of Canada, which he and Randolph had predicted, was half-heartedly under way. But halfhearted or not, the invasion of Canadian soil was not being taken lightly by the British. They began to retaliate by sending raiding parties up Chesapeake Bay.

Frank came in one day, greatly excited. " A British vessel sailed up the Chesapeake last night after dark and landed fifty men. They raided plantations and burned buildings — "

Polly's hand went to her throat. " Where, Frank? "

" Up at the head of the Bay. They landed at Havre de Grace."

" Oh! I was afraid they might be nearby."

" Not yet, but I fear they will be. That's why I'm going to join up."

" You're going to join the Army? " Polly's tone showed her amazement.

Frank nodded emphatically, his lips grim. " It's different, when the enemy is invading your shores and threatening the security of your home and family! George Peter is organizing a company. We have to be ready when Cockburn's boats come south."

" O Frank, the children! "

" Never fear. We won't let Cockburn get inland."

Polly didn't see much of her husband in the next week. He was busy signing papers and getting measured for a new blue uniform. Most of the men who were joining Major Peter's artillery were friends, both of the Major and of each other, young men well established in business or professions in Georgetown. Major Peter was a neighbor of Frank's and a fellow town councilman.

" We'll assign you to an artillery piece, Key," the Major said. " Can you sponge and ram a fieldpiece? "

Frank grinned. " If you give me a fieldpiece, I'm sure I can."

But the excitement was over before Frank got his gun. Cockburn sailed out of the Chesapeake, and there was no longer an immediate need for Peter's artillerymen. However, they couldn't disband so lightly. The President reviewed the company in their new tailored uniforms. They sat their own fine horses and made a very pretty sight. Polly took the older children to see them. Then the company had a big dinner party and went home to their families. They had been in the service of their country just eleven days.

It was almost a year before they were needed again. This time, Rear Admiral Cockburn invaded the Maryland shores in earnest. Major Peter's company hurriedly re-formed. Frank brought out his uniform. " Get your needle, Polly," he said. " I've a little job for you." He wouldn't tell her what it was. He was keeping it for a surprise. When she had come with her needle and thread and thimble, he took an envelope out of his breast pocket.

" What is it you want, Frank? Have you a button off? "

" No, I've some bars off."

" Some what? " She wrinkled her nose at him.

He handed her the envelope. " Your husband is now a lieutenant," he said, smiling broadly.

" Why, Francis Scott Key! And you didn't tell me! "

" *Lieutenant* Francis Scott Key, if you please! "

" And how did all this happen, may I ask? "

" Major Peter wants me to handle supplies. As quartermaster, I rate a lieutenant's rank and a lieutenant's pay."

Polly knew exactly what to do with the bars; her father was a colonel. But Frank didn't know exactly what to do with the job the bars represented. As quartermaster, it was his task to secure supplies for the company. Supplies meant, first of all, horses and wagons; and, secondly, food. He was expected to get both from his neighbors.

He started out bravely enough, riding straight and handsome on the back of a beautiful sorrel from his own stables, followed by two sergeants and half a dozen privates to take care of the provisions he would wheedle out of people.

The first day he didn't keep his men very busy. All of them were friends or acquaintances of long standing, and as they rode through the pleasant June countryside they sang and joked as merrily as if they were on an all-day picnic. But as evening came on, and lengthening shadows told them that they must return to Georgetown and their company, Frank took stock of the day's work and was not pleased.

Hardest of all was the task of getting farmers to give up their work horses. " We need our horses," they told Frank. " Whether the country's at war or peace, people have to eat. If we don't have horses to take care of our crops how can we produce food for your Army? "

Frank could see the logic of their case. He found it much harder to plead the cause of horses, wagons, and food for the Army than to plead a point of law.

Now at the end of the first day they had just two horses, both old and broken down, that had been put out to pasture as unfit for work in the fields. One was almost blind. The other was spavined. But at least they could pull a wagon. The wagon too was a sorry sight. A farmer had pointed it out to them in a draw in one of his fields. " If you can use it, you're welcome," he said. " I figured 'twarn't worth the time to fix it up, but maybe you fellows' time ain't worth much."

Frank bit his tongue and ordered his men to see what they could do with the wagon. There wasn't a carpenter among them, but with the help of the farmer's hammer and nails, his pile of old lumber, and a good bit of his advice, they managed to get it together.

" At least it has four wheels," Sergeant George joked.

They hitched the sad-looking team to the sad-looking

wagon, threw in a few bags of corn and wheat; a side of bacon; and a bushel of early apples that Frank had managed to wheedle out of farmers who refused him horses, and stood staring at the fruit of their day's labor.

One of the privates lifted an eyebrow and drawled, " How long do you reckon the company can eat on today's stores, Lieutenant? "

Frank was disgruntled. " We've got to do better than this tomorrow," he said.

But they didn't do much better. And shortly the Army was ready to march. " We're going up to the Patuxent," Major Peter told Frank. " The British fleet's gone up the river, and Cockburn's raiders are busy along its shores. You'll have to go ahead and forage. If you can't get the farmers to give you food, your men will have to take it. An army on the march has to eat. The men can't go home to their own tables as they've done here in Georgetown."

Frank understood, but he could think of nothing more distasteful than sending his men out to raid as the enemy was doing. Still, if it had to be done, it had to.

" We'll get under way at dawn the day after tomorrow," Major Peter explained. " I want you and your men to precede us by a day. We will meet you here " — he indicated a point on the map — " Wednesday night. Have supplies for a hearty dinner and breakfast. The men will be tired and hungry after their first day out."

Frank managed to have the supplies at the appointed place, but he had not enjoyed his duties. I'm about as good at soldiering, he thought, as I'd be at politics. In fact, I doubt if any of us in the Company would stack up very well as soldiers, except perhaps the Major himself, who's a professional Army man. We're used to living too easily and well. We aren't used to the discipline necessary to an efficient army. Actually, we don't know how either to give commands or to take them. He shook his head as he looked about at his friends stretched out around the campfires laughing and talking. What will happen to us when we meet the enemy? he wondered.

The Company continued up the Patuxent River to Benedict, and Frank secured enough for them to eat, but he was not proud of his job, nor of his methods.

At Benedict they sighted the enemy — three ships in the river, flying the British Jack. On shore they saw the results of enemy plunder. But though they waited in ambush for three days, expecting each night that raiding parties would land from the ships, nothing happened. Had the enemy been warned of their coming? On the fourth morning, the British ships were nowhere to be seen. They had taken advantage of the dawn breeze to sail back down the river into the Bay.

So Major Peter's company started home. They still had to eat, and Frank grimly continued foraging. On the second morning, he and his little band went out before daylight to see what they could rustle. It was discouraging business. Just as the dawn flung banners of pink across the sky, they rode into a farmyard and were met by the owner. Frank steeled himself, expecting to be told to get off the place, but, to his surprise, the man smiled and put out his hand. " You're Frankie Key," he said. " You don't remember me, but I used to stop at Terra Rubra when you were a boy. I'd know you anywhere."

Frank was delighted to meet a friend of his father's, but

he had no time for reminiscing. " I'm surely glad to see you, Sir," he said. " I'm quartermaster for Major Peter's artillery. We've just been up the Patuxent after the enemy, but they escaped us. I'm looking for something to augment our breakfast supplies."

" You've come to the right place. Pull up by my smokehouse yonder, and have your men load up what they need. I've a goodly supply of smoked side meat."

" Thank you, Sir! Thank you very much." Frank's tone carried the depth of his appreciation. He gave the order to his men, then stood talking a moment to his host before following them. As he approached the smokehouse in the early dawn, he was thinking about the time Washington had visited Terra Rubra. If only the Army today had a Washington!

Suddenly something hit him a terrific blow on the side of the head, and he reeled drunkenly. He caught the corner of the wagon to keep from going down, and closed his eyes against the dizziness that came over him. Dimly he heard Sergeant George's voice: " Look out for the Lieutenant! Didn't you see him, you lug? " Then an arm steadied him. " Sit down here, Lieutenant. What a wallop he gave you! "

Frank blinked his eyes open to see the Sergeant bending over him.

" Are you all right, Lieutenant? Morgan hit you with a chunk of side meat he was throwing into the wagon."

Frank's lips twitched in a wry grin. " I'm the Major's prize war casualty if nothing else! Yesterday I fell in the river, and today I get knocked senseless with a side of meat! "

20

RED SKY

Polly must have heard that Major Peter's company was returning, for she was at the door, surrounded by the children, when Frank rode up.

" Hello, Papa! Hello, Papa! " A medley of treble voices greeted him as he dismounted and handed his horse over to a servant. Then he was besieged. Little arms tugged at his trouser legs; longer arms encircled him. Polly stood back and smiled at him over the heads of the children. He picked up the two youngest, and, with one on each shoulder, bent to kiss his wife. " You're prettier than ever," he murmured.

" Papa, your uniform looks awful! Did you fight the enemy? Did you get wounded? " All the questions seemed to be coming from his eldest son.

" No, Frankie, the enemy got away from us. They sailed off down the Bay again."

" Your uniform does look as if it had been through the wars," Polly said, walking into the house at his side.

" I fell in the river," Frank said wryly. " It shrank."

" And faded," Polly said. " But you're hot and tired. Come, children, let your father get cleaned up. Later he can tell us all about what happened."

" There isn't much to tell," Frank said, " except that I've had my fill of being quartermaster."

Polly flashed him an understanding smile, and he went thankfully up the stairs to get out of his sweaty, dirty uniform.

" Do you think you're home for a while now? " Polly asked him that night at dinner.

" There's no telling. You know we're not just an independent troop now. This area's been made the Tenth Military District, with General Winder in command. We're subject to call at any time."

" You'd better get a new uniform ordered at once," Polly said, smiling. " You really were a sorry sight in the old one."

Frank answered her smile, then turned serious. " Polly, I think you should take the children and go to Terra Rubra. Nobody knows, but it seems likely that Cockburn's next raids will be up the Potomac."

Polly's lips parted, and Frank thought she turned a trifle pale. But she said, " I'm not going off and leave you, Frank."

" But, darling, I may not be here. In fact, I most certainly won't be if they come up the Potomac — "

" There seems to be a great deal of talk about an attack on Annapolis or Baltimore."

Frank knew she was thinking about her family at Annapolis. " Personally, I think the enemy's next strike will be at Washington. That's why I want you to get away."

" Even if they attack Washington, why would they bother us in Georgetown? *We*'re not the Capital."

" No, but we're too close to it for comfort. I really think you should go, Polly. Perhaps Taney could come down and get you."

" I'll stay right here as long as you stay," she said stubbornly.

Nevertheless, Frank wrote to Taney. He also started his tailor on another uniform. He wasn't at home much during the remainder of July. Major Peter was doing his best to get his company in shape for action. He drilled them daily, led them into the country on forced marches and in various maneuvers. Frank felt the tension of uncertainty. Waiting was difficult, yet the raw troops desperately needed this time for preparation.

One night in early August he came home to find Taney there. " Roger! " he cried. " I've never been so glad to see anyone. Have you persuaded this stubborn wife of mine that she should return to Frederick with you? "

Taney shook his head. " I'm afraid not," he admitted. " As you say, she *is* stubborn — deuced stubborn."

Frank and his friend talked long into the night. " They'll attack Washington, as sure as I'm alive," Frank said, " but President Madison doesn't think so. So no preparations are being made. He and his Cabinet have the idea that if and when the British do make a major attack, all they have to do is call out the militia. A lot of good they'll be — untrained, unorganized. General Winder has repeatedly asked for more troops, but he doesn't get them."

" I'll tell you what I think," Taney said. " I think the two parties are too busy quarreling to bother with the war. They're more interested in the coming elections than in defending the country."

Frank nodded. " Politics again! " he said. " It's hopeless. I not only think the British will attack the Capital. I think they'll take it. That's why I want to get Polly and the children away. I hate to think what might happen to Georgetown."

But Taney left for home the next day without Frank's family. Polly refused to go.

On a hot Sunday afternoon a few weeks later, when Frank was lounging at home with his family, word came that the British had landed a large force at Benedict.

" Not just raiding parties? Actual troops? " Frank asked the messenger who brought him the news.

" Troops, Lieutenant, and the report is that there are thousands of them. They've been unloading all day."

Frank called for his horse, hurried into his uniform, and grabbed his pistols. He kissed Polly and the children hastily. " General Winder may be planning to march. I must get to my company. I still wish you were safe at Terra Rubra." His eyes were troubled.

" We'll be all right," Polly said stanchly. Then her voice turned tremulous. " Just so you come back to us."

Frank held her close for a moment, then jumped on his horse and was gone. But he did not find the American troops preparing to march against the invading army. They were waiting — waiting to see what the enemy was going to do — waiting to see where they were going to attack! Frank shook his head.

They waited three days, and the waiting to Frank was torture. " Why don't we attack them? Why do we sit here and wait for them to attack us? " he demanded of anyone who would listen. President Madison rode out to where the troops were bivouacked. Secretary of State Monroe rode out. Secretary of War Armstrong rode out. But still they did nothing.

In the meantime, Frank heard that the British had made an encampment at Upper Marlboro and that the top officers — General Ross, Rear Admiral Cockburn, and Vice-Admiral Cochrane — were quartered at the home of Dr. Beanes. " Well, the doctor may not like having them as guests, but I'll venture he's being a perfect host," Frank said. " I envy them. The doctor sets a sumptuous table, and I can think of no place more inviting for an hour's rest than his garden."

" If the General and the Admirals have time for an hour's rest! " someone chimed in. " I've a feeling they're very busy making preparations to rout us."

About ten o'clock on the morning of August 24, a messenger galloped into camp, his horse's sides heaving. " The British are on the march toward Bladensburg! "

Bladensburg was a village just outside Washington. " I knew it all the time," Frank said grimly. " I knew they'd attack the Capital. It was the logical thing — " His voice was lost in the confusion. President Madison rode to the General's tent. Members of the Cabinet rode through the camp giving orders.

" Who the devil's in charge? " Frank demanded.

" The Lord only knows," a lieutenant at his side answered.

" We ought to form right now and go to meet the enemy before they get to Bladensburg," Frank said excitedly.

" Now who thinks he's in charge! " the other lieutenant said sarcastically.

" At least I'm only expressing an opinion, not giving
orders," Frank defended himself.

Out of the confusion it finally became clear that
General Winder *was* trying to get his army formed to
move toward Bladensburg. The blazing sun, added to
the frantic activity, was exhausting. By the time they
were ready to march, the men were jaded. At the head of
the army rode the President and his Cabinet, until noon,
when the enemy was sighted on Lowndes Hill. Then
they fell back, but they did not cease to give orders. Everyone had a different idea as to what should be done,
and everyone must have his say. Frank bit his lip. " Winder's a lawyer, not a general," he said. But as he watched
the bedlam, his sympathies were more and more with the
General. For no more did he get a plan set into motion
than Secretary of State Monroe or some other dignitary
gave commands that counteracted his. " They *can't* keep
this up! " Frank cried. " The enemy will be upon us."

At last came the order, " Advance to meet the enemy! "
Major Peter's artillery, however, were left behind to set
up their guns along the road to Washington. With the
perspiration running down his face, Frank worked desperately with the others to get the six-pounders set. When
they were finally in readiness, he took his place beside his
gun. " Oh, no! " he cried. Directly in range of the cannon was their own Thirty-sixth Regiment, drawn up for
battle. " We'll be firing into our own men! " he shouted.

Major Peter had already discovered the dilemma and
was riding off to see to the removal of the Thirty-sixth,

for it was slow and difficult business to move heavy artillery, and there was no time for that now.

As Frank watched, the Thirty-sixth fell back. Even though Major Peter's artillery was on a slope, Frank could not see far enough toward the Bladensburg bridge to tell what was happening there. But he clearly heard the report of a messenger who rode up to Major Peter shouting: " We cut the first company to pieces, but now the second one's coming across the bridge, and they're hurling rockets — — "

" Man your guns! " Major Peter barked. Soon the guns too were barking, but they were not enough. Frank could see, through the smoke of battle, that the British were coming on. Frantically he sponged and rammed his fieldpiece.

Then suddenly came the command, " Cease fire! " As the smoke cleared, Frank could see the reason for the order. It was not that the Americans had won the day — far from it. They were retreating in broken ranks, fleeing back down the Georgetown road. It was a rout. Frank groaned. The fieldpieces were left upon the hill, and Major Peter's company followed the others, making their way homeward across the fields, trying only to avoid the enemy.

Frank stumbled into his own door late in the afternoon.

Polly had heard the news. " O Frank, you're safe! " she cried.

" Yes, I'm safe," he said, his tone heavy with fatigue and the poignancy of his grief, " but the Capital — they're marching down the streets of the Capital — "

" I know," Polly said.

Frank slumped into the nearest chair, and Polly knelt beside him and held his head against her breast.

After a moment he roused himself. " See that the doors are all bolted," he said, " and the children inside. Georgetown may be next."

" The children are all upstairs," she soothed him. " Mammy Sue's looking after them. I'll tell Tom to see to the doors." She got up to find Tom.

" We must pack," Frank said, the words muted by his hands, which covered his face.

Polly looked over her shoulder at him. Her eyes were compassionate. She did not answer.

After a little he dragged himself to the window. " It looks as if all of Washington is fleeing past our door," he said. " I wonder where the President is." He didn't care too much about Madison personally, but the disgrace of the President and Cabinet having to flee from the Capital shamed him to the core.

" I don't know about Mr. Madison," Polly said, " but I heard that Mrs. Madison refused to leave until the enemy were actually in the streets of the city. When her servants finally got her into her carriage, the only thing she had with her was George Washington's portrait off the wall."

Frank's eyes for a moment turned tender. " Brave little Dolly Madison," he said. " She's worth two of her husband — as you're worth two of yours."

Polly patted his hand. " You'd as well get cleaned up and rest a little," she said.

" Come on up with me. You can be packing. We don't

know what's to come, and you and the children must be ready to go in case they turn on Georgetown. The carriage is ready at a minute's notice. Tom will drive you to Terra Rubra."

Polly humored him, although she thought she must feel exactly as Dolly Madison had felt; she was determined not to leave unless the enemy was actually at her doorstep — and then only for the sake of the children's safety.

Frank changed clothes, then paced the floor. "If only I knew what's going on across the river," he moaned.

When darkness fell, he did know. As he and Polly watched from the conservatory, the eastern sky began to lighten. "Like a false dawn," Polly murmured. Frank's arm about her tightened. The light grew; it was a red light, and it soon seemed to fill the whole sky. The Capital was going up in flames. A dry sob racked Frank's body.

21

A PRISONER

In bitter humiliation, Frank watched the Capital of his country go up in flames. But where man had not interfered, nature did. As he and Polly watched the fire, red against the sky, they heard the rumble of thunder. Frank stepped outside.

"There's a big storm brewing," he said. " Lightning is cleaving the sky like a giant sword blade."

"Frank, a hard rain would put out the fires! "

" I'm afraid it's too late to save the Government buildings."

When the storm struck, it was with the violence of a tornado. The wind whipped the trees into grotesque shapes as Frank and Polly watched from the conservatory. "I'm frightened, Frank," Polly whispered. " It's as if God were taking a hand."

Frank put his arm around her and held her tight, but he could not bring himself to leave the spectacle. It was as if they had box seats — first for the colossal destruction by man, now for the reprisal by God. When a flash of lightning showed them the night without, it seemed not the world they knew, but something out of the regions of darkness. Sheets of rain struck the glass walls of the conservatory with such violence that it seemed the glass must come crashing in on them.

They watched in awe until at last the fury abated. Then Frank gave an ironic chuckle. Polly looked at him in surprise.

" I was just thinking what a drenched and sodden mass the British troops must be. It serves them right — burning all the buildings in Washington — to have nowhere to get in out of the storm! "

The next morning early, there was a messenger at the door for Frank.

" General Winder's reassembling the troops at Montgomery Courthouse, Sir."

Frank had been expecting a call and was ready. " I only wish you and the children were at Terra Rubra," he said to Polly as he kissed her good-by in the dimness of the upper hall. " Remember, if word should come that the enemy is headed for Georgetown, you're to leave instantly."

" I know, dear. We're all packed, and you've told Tom to have the carriage ready."

When Frank reached Montgomery Courthouse, he found a bitter, humiliated General barking orders as if he hated every man in camp, himself included. The orders were passed down the line: " Prepare to defend Annapolis and Baltimore."

These were more orders from Madison and Monroe, Frank felt sure. The General, left to his own devices, would have re-formed his men to make an attack on the enemy now, in the streets of the gutted Capital — would have tried to prevent them from returning to their ships.

No wonder he was bitter! What a farce, Frank thought. Politicians trying to run a war!

The next day he was back with his family, airing his disgust to Polly and the children. " The enemy were right here under our noses. But we let them go back to their ships unmolested, so that they can sail on to Annapolis or Baltimore and make a shambles of another city. At least, the other cities won't have the President and his Cabinet on hand to give them orders, so perhaps they can defend themselves with more success. Anyway, I won't worry about you so much now, here in Georgetown."

There was an imperative summons at the door, and Frank jumped up to follow the servant into the hall. As the door opened, he saw that it was his friend Richard West disheveled and excited, who had pounded so imperiously.

" West! " he exclaimed. " What is it? "

" It's Dr. Beanes — "

." What about him? "

" Taken prisoner by the British — "

" Taken prisoner? I thought he'd been playing host to their high and mighty. Why would they take him prisoner? " Frank's anger, which had been building up for days and weeks, suddenly pinpointed on the British high command. " Fine thanks for his hospitality! " he exploded. " What do they mean? An old man and a gentleman like Dr. Beanes. Come into the study. Now, what's it all about? "

" The officers had left Dr. Beanes's house to go back to the fleet. I guess Dr. Beanes was enjoying the treat of having his home to himself again. He was entertaining a couple of old cronies in the garden when a noisy disturbance in the streets interrupted them. Well, you know how Dr. Beanes thinks everything that goes on in Upper Marlboro is his business — "

Frank nodded. " I know."

" So he sent his servants to find out what was going on. They reported it was British soldiers making merry — a few stragglers that hadn't gotten on their way with the main body of troops — "

" Yes, yes. Go on."

" So the doctor ordered them thrown in jail for disturbing the peace."

" No! " Frank exclaimed. " Surely he knew better than to do that! "

" Knew better, no doubt, but didn't do better. He's used to being a dictator in Upper Marlboro, you know. He didn't foresee the consequences of meddling with something out of his jurisdiction."

" So they took him prisoner! "

" Evidently he didn't get all the stragglers jailed, for someone reported the situation to the General, and he sent a detachment back to release the prisoners and take Dr. Beanes."

" When was this? "

" Last night about midnight. They hardly gave the doctor time to get his clothes on. The report is that he's not to be exchanged as an ordinary prisoner. They took him aboard their flagship. I've come to get you to go plead for him."

" Me? " Frank asked in surprise.

His visitor nodded. " His friends felt you would be the best person to go."

" I'm willing to do anything I can, of course. But why *me?* Why not someone from Upper Marlboro? "

Mr. West smiled. " Because you're a very winsome pleader, Mr. Key. This is not an ordinary job for an ordinary man. Your ability to use words persuasively — "

" I see. I'll go, of course." His brows were drawn together in thought. Where should he start?

" Thank you! Thank you very much, Mr. Key. The citizens of Upper Marlboro will be greatly in your debt. Our prayers go with you." He extended his hand.

Frank took it absently. " The President," he murmured. " Wherever he is — I'll go to him."

The visitor bowed himself out and Frank went to work.

" I'll have to get a release from duty, from General Winder; permission from the President to approach the British fleet under a flag of truce — " He called Polly to tell her the news, then mounted his horse and set out. He found that the President had returned from his flight and had set up temporary headquarters in a private home in Washington. He rode there immediately, feeling a physical sickness at sight of the blackened ruins where the Capitol had stood, the Hall of Representatives, the War Office, the great library which Jefferson had started. He thought he could not have forced himself to ride through the piteous ruins had not his errand been so urgent.

He was in no mood to listen to the President's plans for defeating the enemy at Annapolis. " I have an errand, Sir," he said at once, " that needs your immediate sanction." Briefly he told the story of Dr. Beanes's capture and imprisonment. " I didn't know where to find Secretary Monroe, and, anyway, I felt that perhaps I should have your personal permission to approach the enemy fleet under a flag of truce."

" You have it," President Madison said. " I've sent General Winder to Annapolis to prepare the defenses there. You should get a letter from him as our Commander. You should also see Colonel Skinner, who is in charge of exchange of prisoners. Perhaps he can accompany you."

" Thank you, Sir. Then if you will excuse me, I shall proceed at once."

" Certainly. May your mission be successful."

Frank had been thinking fast since he left home two hours before. He had no idea how long he would be away on this errand, but it might well be several weeks. This time he was going to insist that Polly go to Terra Rubra. Even though he was no longer afraid of an attack on Georgetown, there was the possibility of unpleasant incidents from stragglers; besides, this would be a good opportunity for Polly to take a little vacation. He would put it up to her that way, and promise to come to Terra Rubra himself when he had finished this job.

" How did you make out? " Polly asked eagerly when he arrived home.

" So far so good. I'll soon be on my way, and so will you." He caught her hands and smiled down on her.

" You don't mean I'm going with you? " she gasped.

Frank laughed. " Of course not, but it looks as though I'd be gone for two or three weeks, and I *would* like to have you take the children and go to Terra Rubra. Then when I finish with this, I'll come down too. I think we need a little vacation in the country after all the excitement."

" All right, Frank."

" That's my good girl."

" I'll really be glad to go," she said with a sigh. " I just didn't want to be away when I knew you'd be coming in tired and discouraged. Now you won't be coming in."

" No, we're sure of that."

When he had his family off, Frank galloped in haste to Annapolis. No one knew where the British fleet might be off to. The sooner he could get started in pursuit of the Admiral's flagship, the better. When he arrived at Headquarters, he found General Winder sympathetic. " I'll write a letter for you to General Ross," he said.

" Thank you, Sir. I'll pick it up in the morning."

He went on to find Colonel John Skinner, whom he had not met. Colonel Skinner had already heard of the plight of Dr. Beanes.

" I can't get him exchanged, for they don't consider him an ordinary prisoner of war," he said. " But I've negotiated with General Ross and Admiral Cockburn on several occasions. Since they know me, I might be of some service. I'll be glad to go with you."

Frank found this man who was to be his companion a likable chap, though a little rough, and inclined to be blunt.

" I know the doctor," he said, " a fine old man. We'll go to Baltimore and get my cartel boat. It's carried me to the enemy fleet before. But wait! Wouldn't it be good strategy to get letters from some of the wounded British officers old Dr. Beanes took care of? "

" Splendid! "

" It may take us a couple of days to make ready, but I don't think we need to worry about the British fleet starting off to England in the meantime."

" I doubt it," Frank agreed with a smile.

22

WITH HIS MAJESTY'S FLEET

The following morning, Frank picked up the letter from General Winder on his way to meet Colonel Skinner.

"I got four letters," Skinner greeted him, "from wounded British officers the doctor treated."

"Good! Then are we ready to leave for Baltimore?"

"I am if you are."

"In that case, we're off."

It was the first day of September, and summer heat was still upon them, so they couldn't push their horses. Frank's impatience was difficult for him to control. "I brought some clean linens for the doctor," he said, running his handkerchief under his own collar to remove the dust. "You know how fastidious he is."

"Humph!" Skinner grunted.

Frank saw that his companion made no effort to keep the dust wiped from his face and neck. No, he wouldn't think clean linen important!

When they reached Baltimore, they rode directly to the water front. The city was a frenzy of activity.

"*They*'re really preparing a defense!" Frank exclaimed. It was just as he had thought. The enemy would not find it so easy to take Baltimore! " Look at those earthworks! " he cried jubilantly.

" Wait till you see Fort McHenry," Skinner replied. " Man, they've some real guns mounted! "

However, Frank did not feel that they should delay to inspect the defenses of Baltimore. " If your craft is ready, I think we should be off at once," he said.

" It's always ready," Skinner said brusquely. " Come along."

They left their horses and Skinner strode down the wharf, Frank following. Soon he stopped before a small, nondescript-looking craft. " Be ready to put off within the hour! " Skinner barked at the sailors aboard her.

So this was the cartel boat! Frank could see no name, no number, on her sides.

The sailors began at once to hoist the mast.

" It's a good time to be off," Skinner said. " The wind is with us."

Frank felt a mounting excitement. He was going to board this small, trim vessel and skim down the Chesapeake in search of the British fleet. He was going to attempt to wrest his friend from the Admiral of the fleet. And from what he had heard of Cockburn, he was a bully and a devil. It was likely that General Ross would also be aboard. He hoped so. He understood that Ross was a gentleman.

" The fleet's still reported near the mouth of the Potomac," Skinner said. " That means we've a hundred-mile trip ahead of us unless they come to meet us."

" I wonder what they're waiting for," Frank mused as they went aboard the cartel. " If they're going to attack

Annapolis or Baltimore, you'd think they'd be about it."

A few minutes later, Skinner stood beside Frank on the foreward deck. " We're ready to put off," he said.

The little craft began to move, and Frank felt a tingling of anticipation. He was much happier about this kind of assignment than one as quartermaster or artilleryman. He realized the difficulty of the task before him, yet he felt only eagerness to be at it.

" How long will it take us? " he asked Skinner.

" Several days. How many depends on the wind."

" Look! " Frank exclaimed in sudden excitement.

" Yes, I was going to tell you that you'd get a good view of Fort McHenry from out here on the river."

Actually, however, it wasn't the fortification itself, but the flag flying over it that had caused Frank's exclamation. " I've never seen such a huge flag! " he cried. The light breeze that was catching the sails of their boat and skimming it smoothly down the Patapsco was also catching the folds of an immense flag which flew over Fort McHenry, rippling them out until the banner seemed to lie flat against the sky like a mammoth picture painted on a vast, pale-blue background. Emotion surged up in Frank. The American flag had always touched off a flame of love and patriotism in his heart as nothing else could do. " It's the most beautiful thing I've ever seen," he murmured, his voice husky. " Those broad stripes — those bright stars — — "

" They say it's thirty-six feet long and twenty-nine feet wide," Skinner said in a matter-of-fact voice, " the biggest flag ever made on this continent. A Mrs. Pickersgill and her daughter were commissioned to make the banner by General Stricker and Commodore Barney."

Frank scarcely heard. *The star-spangled flag of our nation,* he was thinking. He caught Skinner's word " banner " and altered the line to include it: *The star-spangled banner,* he said to himself. Polly would like that. She had liked the other line, and this was better. He felt choked with emotion as he stood watching the flag until a bend in the river cut it off from view.

When they were out of the Patapsco and in the Bay, Frank felt that they were really on their way. He found Skinner an interesting companion. Polly would call him a " common man," he thought, smiling to himself, and she would mean no disrespect by the term. She would mean only that he did not belong in the " gentleman " class with her husband and his friends. Skinner was patriotic, and he was capable. One of the odd things he had discovered about him was that he had vague literary ambitions. He's a fellow of strange contradictions, he thought, but at least our literary interests give us something in common.

It was on the morning of the fifth day that Skinner sighted the British fleet, just starting up the Bay.

" They were long enough getting started," Frank commented, " but they're on their way at last."

" I wonder whether they're headed for Annapolis or Baltimore," Skinner said, still scanning the fleet through his glass. " Run up our flag! " he ordered his seamen.

Frank watched the white flag go up.

Then Skinner turned to him. " Would you like a look at His Majesty's fleet? " he said, a curl of sarcasm on his lips.

Frank looked through the glass and felt his heart begin to hammer. It was a beautiful sight, but frightening too. To think that the United States in her immaturity and ignorance would attempt to fight anything so stanch and experienced! Yet what of the Revolution? This new country was even newer then. It was a matter of spirit, he decided. In the Revolution, the Colonies had the will to win, and with that spirit they succeeded. If only something could give spirit to the present army! What would do it? A Commander like George Washington. But there seemed to be no such man in sight. What then?

He was still thinking about this, when Skinner hailed the Admiral's flagship, *The Tonnant*. Skinner's craft was recognized at once, and a seaman was sent down the ladder to the cartel boat.

" Sir Alexander Cochrane invites Colonel Skinner and his companion to come aboard," the messenger said, saluting smartly.

" Give him our thanks and tell him we accept his invitation," Skinner said.

The man went back up the ladder.

" I'm glad he's joined them. He's Commander in Chief, and a better man to deal with than Cockburn."

" Good." Frank picked up the bundle he had brought for the doctor and followed their escort up the rope ladder to *The Tonnant*. He had never been on a large vessel before, let alone one belonging to the British Navy, and he found himself as excited as a boy.

They were conducted to the Admiral's cabin, and Skinner made the introductions.

" It's the hour for officers' mess," the Admiral said.

" Rear Admiral Cockburn, General Ross, and I should be happy to have you dine with us."

" Thank you," Skinner said.

" We should be honored," Frank added, bowing to his host.

Frank found the meal delicious and the company most pleasant, except for that of Cockburn.

When they had finished eating, Admiral Cochrane looked at his guests and said, " Now, gentlemen, your business."

Frank looked at Skinner, and Skinner said, " I am not here on the usual routine exchange of prisoners."

He stopped, and Frank knew that the time had come: It was up to him to present his case. He felt the pulses beating in his temples, and he prayed that he might say the right thing. He looked at Cochrane, at Ross, at Cockburn, before he spoke. Then he said, " We've come in behalf of Dr. Beanes, the well-loved and highly respected citizen of Upper Marlboro, whom we understand you are holding through some misunderstanding."

Instantly the atmosphere at the table changed. No longer were the British officers affable hosts. They became hostile enemies. It's as if I were suddenly facing three entirely different men, Frank thought.

" There is no misunderstanding." Ross spoke in brittle tones.

" We felt that there must be," Frank said, " knowing Dr. Beanes as we do to be a highly honorable gentleman, and knowing that he was your very generous host so short a time ago."

" No mistake! " Cockburn cut in with a snarl.

He's the mean one, Frank thought, recalling how it had been reported that General Ross had held out against burning and sacking the Capital, but Cockburn had insisted, and reveled in the destruction.

But all three men were against him now, a solid wall. What was it that made them so bitter toward good Dr. Beanes? He must try to find out. However, before he had time to frame a question to draw them out, Cochrane spoke: " He broke faith with us," he said, and his words cut.

" Surely he did not mean to," Frank said quietly.

" We treated him honorably," General Ross explained. " We gave orders that his property should in no way be harmed. Then the minute we were out of sight, he turned on our men."

" Hangin'd be too good for him," Cockburn bellowed.

" I'm sure his was a thoughtless act rather than a deliberately hostile one," Frank said. " If you knew the doctor as we know him, you would understand that he is used to his word being law in Upper Marlboro. He was simply annoyed and he put a stop to the annoyance."

Cockburn pushed back from the table and stalked to the door. " Thinks he's a king, does he? " he snorted.

" We have more pressing business to attend to," General Ross said, and he also rose. " If you will excuse us — "

Admiral Cochrane was a little more civil. " We will talk with you gentlemen further in the morning."

Colonel Skinner extended his packet of letters to Gen-

eral Ross. " Will you give these your consideration in
the meantime? They are letters from your own wounded
officers."

" And may I please have permission to visit Dr. Beanes
and take him a change of linen that I brought? " Frank
asked.

" I see no reason for granting such a request," Cockburn said, and stalked out.

Frank could feel antagonism hanging in the air, but
Admiral Cochrane said, " I suppose you may see him,"
and called a man to take him to the doctor.

Frank's heart was sick within him, yet he would not
admit defeat. There was still a chance as long as they
had been granted another interview.

He was aghast when he saw the doctor. He was a piti-
ful sight, dirty and unkempt, thrown in with sailors and
soldiers who treated him with the utmost disrespect. His
joy at seeing his friends was heartbreaking. — " I *have* to
get him released," Frank found himself saying over and
over as he went back to the cartel boat. " I have to. I
have to."

He didn't sleep much that night, though the small vessel, tied to *The Tonnant*, rocked gently. He tried to fig-
ure out what appeal would have the best chance against
the hard shell of resistance about the three officers. Should
he tell them that Dr. Beanes had been opposed to the
war? Tell them that he did not approve the invasion of
Canada? Or continue to plead his innocence as a gentleman? Or should he pick up the plea of the letters and
ask for clemency for the good doctor because of his kind
treatment of the British wounded? Perhaps that would

be best, if he could use this conduct as proof of the doctor's good intentions and his gentleman's honor.

He could see no change in the attitude of the three officers when he and Skinner met them in the morning, and
his heart fell. But he noticed that General Ross held the
letters.

" You have read the letters from your wounded officers? " he asked.

The General nodded brusquely.

" I am sure that they speak more eloquently than I
can of the doctor's good intentions and his inability to be
other than a true gentleman," Frank said with feeling.

General Ross did not unbend. " Dr. Beanes deserves
much more punishment than he has received," he said,
" but I feel myself bound to make a return for the kindness that he showed my wounded officers. Upon that
ground, and that only, I will release him."

A flood of relief and gratitude rushed through Frank.
" Thank you, Sir. Thank you very much," he said.

" And now we must inform you," Admiral Cochrane
said, " that you two gentlemen as well as Dr. Beanes must
remain with our fleet for the time being. We are on our
way to attack Baltimore, as you may have surmised, and
can't let you go ashore to give warning of our approach."

Frank could feel the blood drain from his face. Yet they
had known that the fleet was preparing to attack somewhere, and surely Baltimore was the best prepared of
any place on the Maryland shore.

But Cochrane was still speaking. " I'm sorry not to be
able to entertain you gentlemen aboard my ship, but as
you can see, it is already crowded with General Ross's

officers. I'll have you taken aboard my son's ship, *The Surprise.*"

"And Dr. Beanes?" Frank asked.

"He may accompany you," the Admiral said, but Frank caught the note of hostility in his voice. He wished it were possible to depart from the fleet with the doctor at once.

"Thank you, Sir," he said. He bowed and turned to the door.

"So it's Baltimore!" Skinner hissed in his ear as they left the cabin.

"Baltimore," Frank said, seeing again the mammoth flag over the Fort. "God save it!"

23

"O SAY, CAN YOU SEE"

We abandon ship! " Frank said half jocularly as he and Dr. Beanes watched from the deck of *The Surprise* while Skinner, under a British guard, directed the removal of the sails from the cartel boat. The sails were hoisted onto *The Surprise*, and the small crew from the cartel boat, followed by Skinner and the guard, came up the side. Now there was nothing to do but wait.

Dr. Beanes's voice was husky when he spoke. " To think you two are here because of me! You'd better have let them do what they would with me."

Frank cast him an affectionate glance. " This isn't such a bad place to be," he said. " I'm not much of a soldier anyhow. And to have a box seat with the enemy will be an experience unique in history, one to tell our grand-children about! "

The doctor shook his head. " Unique, but hardly desirable," he said.

The waiting became long, and with each day Frank felt the tension mounting within him. One day; two; three; four, they waited, aboard *The Surprise*. There was activity aplenty for everyone else, but none for the three

Americans. Only waiting. How much longer? Frank asked himself, pacing the deck.

Sunday morning he was on deck early, and he saw at once that the fleet was moving toward the mouth of the Patapsco. There was a good breeze, and they were under full sail. In the bright morning sun the white sails glistened. There were about forty ships in the fleet, as near as he could tell. They looked like a flock of giant sea gulls bobbing on the waves.

But what of Baltimore? — Baltimore, these great birds are coming to swoop down and devour you unless you have the strength of eagles. I pray God that you may have that strength. — He hurried below to tell Dr. Beanes and Colonel Skinner the news.

" If the wind holds, we'll reach North Point today," Skinner said, when he and Dr. Beanes reached the rail.

" Do you think that means an attack today? " Frank asked. His muscles were tense; he gripped the rail with both hands.

" I doubt it. Tomorrow perhaps."

After the ignominious burning of the Capital, it seemed to Frank that Baltimore *must* stand. " What's to become of us," he said under his breath to the two at his side, " if we lose Baltimore? Are we to lose the war? Go back to being British subjects? " His voice was bitter.

" Baltimore won't be another Washington. She'll put up a fight. You could see that when we were there," Skinner replied, his voice low.

" Polly's sister — " Frank murmured.

" What about your wife's sister? " Dr. Beanes asked.

" She and her family live in Baltimore. Her husband,

Judge Nicholson — Captain Nicholson, I suppose I should say — is second in command at the Fort. I was thinking about the women and children, if the enemy should take the city."

Dr. Beanes shook his head sadly.

The wind held, and by midafternoon *The Surprise* was putting down anchor off North Point.

" We're about ten miles from Fort McHenry," Skinner said.

" What do you suppose they're going to do? " Frank asked anxiously.

" Send reconnoitering parties ashore," Skinner replied, peering over the side, his hand shading his eyes against the sun. " Watch for the small boats to be lowered."

" I'm surprised no one pays any attention to us," Dr. Beanes said.

" They know our hands are tied," Skinner replied.

" I'd like to swim ashore and warn them in Baltimore," Frank said fiercely, clenching his hands into fists.

Skinner laughed. " If we tried to get off this ship, we'd soon find we were being watched."

" I know," Frank said. " Look! There go boats over the side now! "

Skinner nodded. " They'll seek out the lay of the land tonight, and tomorrow will be the day."

Frank began to pace the deck. His anxiety was almost more than he could endure.

Before dawn the next morning there was a knock on the door of the cabin that the three Americans shared. Frank was awake on the instant. He leaped from his bunk. " Yes? "

" Orders from Admiral Cochrane. The Americans will prepare to return to the cartel boat at once."

" Did you hear? " Frank shouted to the others. But they were already getting into their clothes.

" So our box seat's to be on our own vessel," Skinner said.

There seemed to be a great deal of commotion on *The Surprise* as the three went above. Frank craned his neck, trying to see what it was. Just as they were lowered over the side, he discovered: Rear Admiral Cochrane and his staff were boarding *The Surprise*.

" So *The Surprise* is to be the flagship," Skinner remarked.

" And we're to be tied to her like a tail on a kite," Frank said.

" If only we could know what's going on," Dr. Beanes fretted.

" I've a feeling that more than reconnoitering parties have gone ashore," Skinner said dryly.

Frank shot him a quick glance. " Land forces? " he asked.

" We'll soon know."

It wasn't long before the sound of gunfire on shore brought the three men quickly to the deck of the cartel.

" It's a battle! " Frank cried.

" As I thought." Skinner seized the telescope and scanned the shore. " You can't see a thing," he said in anguish.

All day the sound of firing came to them intermittently. " If only we could know how it's going! " Frank exclaimed.

" We'll know nothing till it's over one way or another," Skinner said.

" That could be weeks," Frank said, " if they lay siege to the city."

" It could that," Dr. Beanes agreed.

No one on the cartel slept much that night. As soon as the dawn wind broke, Frank felt a tug at the boat, like the pull of a fish on a line. " We're under sail! " he cried.

" Then we're heading for Fort McHenry," Skinner said.

A sound like a sob came from the doctor.

" The Fort's defended to a T," Frank reassured him. " We saw it as we came out. And they're flying the most tremendous flag! It won't be easy to defeat a garrison with such spirit."

They hurried on deck. Frank saw at once that *The Surprise* had changed its position in the fleet. It was bringing up the rear. " They're protecting their Admiral," he said dryly.

" Lucky for us," Skinner said. " If they'd left us in front, we might easily have been the victims of our own guns."

As daylight began to spread over the world, the watchers on the cartel boat could see that the British armada was fanning out in a semicircle, facing Fort McHenry. And there was the flag! The star-spangled flag flying over the Fort! Frank's throat ached with emotion.

Then suddenly the first gun from the fleet boomed forth its sound and fury.

" They've opened fire! " Frank cried, as if the others didn't know.

The first volley was followed by another and another. The cartel boat began to toss as the concussion of the big guns rocked the frigates.

Frank seized the telescope and watched the bombs trace their fiery route against the sky, dark with clouds and smoke. " All you can see is bombs bursting," he cried. " You can't tell what damage they're doing. Isn't the Fort firing back? "

" They're firing," Skinner said. " Listen carefully and you'll hear their guns between volleys from the fleet. They're not wasting ammunition, though. I doubt that the fleet's in their range."

" I hear them! " Frank exclaimed. The sound of the American guns cheered him. " Why doesn't the fleet move in closer? " He had to shout to make himself heard over the din of battle.

He saw Skinner's lips twist into a grimacing half-smile as he shook his head. " *They* don't want to get within range of our guns," he shouted back.

As the sky grew darker, it was only with a flash of shell-fire that the flag was visible over the Fort. Each time Frank saw it he said, " Thank God.

" And thank God they made such a huge flag, or we'd never be able to see it," he added to the others when a bursting bomb lighted the flag as if a floodlight had searched it out.

" It's going to storm," Dr. Beanes said.

Now to the fireworks of battle were added sharp peals of thunder and brilliant streaks of lightning.

Finally the three men were driven below. But when the thunderstorm was over, Frank hurried back on deck.

The bombardment continued through the enveloping black shroud of night. He could see nothing but the red burst of flame from the guns.

After a time Skinner joined him.

" Where's the doctor? " Frank asked.

" Resting. He sent me up for you. He says you and I should get some rest too."

Frank turned to follow Skinner below and realized that his teeth were chattering.

He couldn't stay below for long. His agonizing anxiety was eased somewhat when he could see the spurts of gunfire that told him the Fort had not surrendered. He went back on deck.

As the long night wore on, the three men shuttled back and forth: up to the deck; below to their cabin; up and down; up and down.

They were all below, and Frank had thrown himself momentarily on his bunk when something made him sit bolt upright. " They've ceased firing! " he cried, his voice loud in the stillness. He ran for the deck. The sailors were already there. " What's happened? " Frank demanded.

No one knew. The firing had ceased; that was all.

" Do you think the Fort's surrendered? " Frank asked.

" There's no way to know till dawn shows us whether the flag's still there," Dr. Beanes said, his voice unsteady.

The flag! Oh, to know if the flag was still flying! Frank pulled an envelope out of his pocket, and in the darkness scrawled something on it with a stub of a pencil.

" What time is it? " Skinner asked.

Dr. Beanes struck a match and held it to the face of his

big gold watch. " Half after three," he said.

" And still cloudy," Frank said with a sigh.

" It was after five yesterday morning before you could see your hand in front of your face."

" Two hours yet! " Frank began to pace the deck.

They waited, thinking every moment the bombardment might again begin, but there was only silence.

" The silence is worse than the guns," Frank said.

They paced. They looked at their watches. They peered at the sky.

" Listen! " Frank said at last. He strained his ears. Surely that was the sound of oars!

" It's a landing party! A big one! " Skinner exclaimed. " They're going beyond the Fort and attack from the rear! "

" Oh, no! " Frank moaned. " What time is it now? "

This time Skinner answered. " Ten minutes past four."

Frank looked to see what the doctor was doing and discovered he was at the telescope. " Can you see anything? " he demanded.

" No," the doctor admitted.

At five o'clock, Frank went to the telescope and would not leave.

" Can you see it? " the others kept asking. " Can you see the flag? "

" Not yet."

" The darkness is thinning," Dr. Beanes murmured.

" What time? " Frank asked.

" Five fifteen."

Then there was silence. Frank strained his eyes through the gray dawn. Suddenly he said uncertainly, " I think I

see it." Then he let out a shout of joy: " I do! I know I
do! It's still there! The flag is still flying! "

He handed the telescope over to Skinner, snatched
envelope and pencil from his pocket, and squatting on
the deck with the envelope on his knee, he began to write:

> " O say, can you see,
> By the dawn's early light — "

Dimly Frank heard the jubilant voices of his compan-
ions, but loud and clear he heard the words that his fingers raced to pencil on the envelope. There wasn't
enough room. He tore the envelope open and continued
to write on the other side.

He heard Dr. Beanes say, " Where's Frank? "

" Over there," Skinner said.

" Whatever's he doing? "

" Writing. I'd let him alone if I were you." Suddenly
Skinner's voice changed. " Look! " he shouted. " The
landing party we heard leaving the fleet — they're scur-
rying back to the ships! "

Frank sprang to his feet. " What? " he cried.

" The land forces have been driven back! "

They stood at the rail. The sun was just coming up,
and as it broke through a rift in the clouds, it fell full on
the flag over the Fort. Frank choked with emotion. The
British land forces were scuttling back to the fleet; the
American flag was still flying! He put his envelope against
the rail and went back to his writing. The guns of the
fleet had opened fire again, but they would not prevail
against the Fort!

" Anybody have a piece of paper? " His envelope was full.

Skinner pulled out a letter. " Here, take this."

The voices of the others were background music as he wrote.

" They're weighing anchor! "

" They're turning tail."

There was a hail from the British sailors aboard *The Surprise*.

" They're handing down our sails and cutting us loose."

" *The Surprise* is turning. The fleet's retreating! "

It had been growing darker and darker, and now it began to rain again. Skinner and the sailors were busy with the sails. Frank and Dr. Beanes went below.

After a time Skinner joined them. " Well, we're under sail for Baltimore. The proud British armada has turned tail and run! "

Frank had been busy with his pencil again. He looked up, and his eyes were bright. " Dr. Beanes, you're a free man," he said. " Thank God, we're all alive and able to return to ' the land of the free and the home of the brave.' "

Skinner looked at him with interest. " Is that a line of the poem you've been writing? " he asked.

Frank nodded. " I don't have it quite finished." He went back to his smudged paper, marking out a word, chewing his pencil, supplying another word.

At last Skinner came to say the cartel was approaching the wharf.

" I'm ready for a bed and a good night's sleep," said Dr. Beanes. " Won't you two be my guests at the Fountain Inn? "

" I have business to attend to first," Skinner said. " You two go on, and I'll join you there later."

Frank took the doctor's arm. " I'm so proud of Baltimore! " he said as they plodded wearily through the streets. " I wonder about casualties." He asked a boy where he could get a paper.

" There ain't none, Sir," the urchin said. " Been no papers for a couple weeks. People's been too busy."

" What of the casualties? " he asked at the inn.

" Negligible," their host answered. " You see, we'd sunk the hulls of a lot of old boats in the harbor, so the British ships couldn't get close enough to hurt us much." He chuckled.

" So that's why the fleet didn't go in closer! We kept wondering," Frank said.

What a splendid defense Baltimore had made! He would like to see his brother-in-law and hear the details, but that would have to wait until morning.

As soon as they had eaten, Dr. Beanes said, " Now for that bed." He and Skinner were soon snoring, but not Frank. He sat by a small table, clean sheets of white paper spread before him, ink and pen at hand, a shaded candle throwing a soft circle of light about him. He pulled the smudged envelopes from his pocket and began neatly copying the words from them onto the clean sheets. He felt a keen excitement. I believe it's good, he thought. Perhaps, if it's good enough, it will inspire other cities to take up the defense of the country as Baltimore did. We can defeat the British if only we try, if only we have the will. We can drive them from our shores and be done with this war.

He changed a word here, a phrase there, as he copied his poem. Occasionally the quiet of the room was broken by the crackling of a sheet of paper he crumpled.

Finally there were four sheets, each with a six-line stanza and a two-line refrain penned in Frank's neat hand. He stacked them together, and across the top of the first wrote: " Tune — ' To Anacreon in Heaven.' "

The words sang in his mind like a refrain. Perhaps others would sing them. He seemed to hear the words swelling and swelling as if a vast multitude were singing them.

It was past midnight, and every bone in his body ached, but he was blissfully content. He blew out the candle, stumbled to his bed, fell on it without removing his clothes, and was instantly asleep.

24

FULFILLMENT

Frank slept deeply until dawn. Then suddenly he was wide awake. " I'm going to leave you gentlemen," he said as soon as the doctor and Skinner were stirring. " I'm off to hunt my brother-in-law." He picked up the sheets of paper from the table.

" I don't know how to thank you, Frank, for what you've done for me," Dr. Beanes said huskily.

" You don't need to thank me. If it hadn't been for our stirring experience, I would never have written this." He patted the white sheets. He was smiling. He felt exhilarated in spite of his short night's sleep.

" I'm very curious," Skinner said. " Aren't you going to read us the poem? "

" Oh," Frank said, " I'm sorry. I guess I'm excited."

He began to read aloud:

" O say, can you see, by the dawn's early light,
  What so proudly we hailed at the twilight's last
     gleaming,
  Whose broad stripes and bright stars, through the peril-
     ous fight,

O'er the ramparts we watched were so gallantly
    streaming?
And the rocket's red glare, the bomb bursting in
    air,
Gave proof through the night that our flag was
    still there!

" O say, does that Star-spangled Banner yet wave
O'er the land of the free and the home of the brave?

" On the shore, dimly seen through the mists of the deep,
    Where the foe's haughty host in dread silence reposes,
What is that which the breeze, o'er the towering steep,
    As it fitfully blows, half conceals, half discloses?
        Now it catches the gleam of the morning's first
        beam,
        In full glory reflected, now shines in the stream.

" 'Tis the Star-spangled Banner, O long may it wave
O'er the land of the free and the home of the brave!

" And where is that band who so vauntingly swore
    That the havoc of war and the battle's confusion
A home and a country should leave us no more?
    Their blood has washed out their foul footsteps'
        pollution;
        No refuge could save the hireling and slave
        From the terror of flight, or the gloom of the grave.

" And the Star-spangled Banner in triumph shall wave
O'er the land of the free and the home of the brave!

" O thus be it ever when freemen shall stand
   Between their loved home and the war's desolation;
Blest with vict'ry and peace, may the heaven-rescued
      land
   Praise the Power that hath made and preserved us a
      nation!
      Then conquer we must, when our cause it is just,
      And this be our motto: ' In God Is Our Trust! '

" And the Star-spangled Banner in triumph shall wave
O'er the land of the free and the home of the brave! "

There was silence when he finished reading. He looked from one to the other.

Dr. Beanes was the first to speak. " It's a stirring piece, Frank." His voice was hoarse with emotion.

Skinner nodded. His eyes were warm. " You've got it captured," he said, " the way it made you feel. What are you going to do with it? "

" I thought I'd take it to my brother-in-law, Judge Nicholson. I have to see him and find out about the family before I leave for Terra Rubra, and I'll see what he thinks about the poem."

" You wrote it for a song? "

" It's singable. I wrote it to that old tune, ' To Anacreon in Heaven.' "

He carefully pocketed the poem, then shook hands with the others. " Probably three men never shared a stranger experience," he said. " I'm sure there will always be a very special bond between us. Good-by for a time, Doctor; I'll see you at Upper Marlboro. Skinner, our paths will no doubt cross again in the duties of war."

"May the war be short-lived," Dr. Beanes said fervently.

Frank left them then and went in search of his brother-in-law.

"He went home to his family last night," a soldier told him. "You might find him there now if you hurry."

It was still early, and Frank set out immediately for the Nicholsons'.

"Frank! Whatever brings you here?" Polly's sister demanded when he was shown in. "You weren't with the troops, were you?"

"No, I was on a special mission."

The Judge was still there. He wrung Frank's hand. "Come have breakfast with us," he said.

As they ate, Frank told them the strange tale of his adventure. Then he drew the folded sheets from his breast pocket. "I wrote this poem about it. Nothing short of hanging could have stopped me. I've never before been so driven to write anything. If you've time before you start for the Fort, I wish you'd glance through it."

The Judge took it, and as he read, Frank watched his face closely. He held deep respect for this brother-in-law's judgment, and as he waited, his heart began to pound. Why am I so concerned? he wondered. I've never taken a poem so seriously before.

The Judge did not look up until he had finished. His eyes were shining. "Frank!" he cried. "It's splendid! Far better than anything you've written before. We must have some copies struck off at once. This could be the very thing to stir the country to victory! "

" Do you think so? " The excitement in the Judge's voice brought an answering vibration to Frank's. Both men had jumped up from the table.

" We'll take it to the Baltimore *American* and have them run off some copies. We'll do it at once. They can get along without me a few minutes longer at the Fort." He kissed his wife. " I should be back tonight," he said.

Frank told his sister-in-law good-by and reached for his cap. " Polly will be so glad to hear you're all safe," he said.

" And how glad she'll be to see you! "

" And I her. Good-by."

" Good-by."

" Will we find anyone at the *American*? " Frank asked as they stepped into the Judge's carriage. " They told me last night there'd been no papers printed for a fortnight."

" We may not, but we'll go see. I'm extremely anxious to see your song distributed at once. We need it. People should be singing it everywhere."

The office was open when they reached it, but there was only a boy there, who said his name was George Sands. " I'm the only one here," he explained. " Everybody else is still in the garrisons or somewhere. Wasn't it a great battle? "

" That it was, Son," the Judge agreed. " And here's a great poem about it. I want very much to get some copies of it run off at once. Do you think you could do it? "

" Well, I've set some type, Sir. I'd be willing to try."

" Good! How long will it take you? "

He shook his head. " I'm pretty slow, but I don't have

anything else to do. I'll get to work on it right away."

" Can you do it today? This gentleman's anxious to be off for home, and I'm eager to see this distributed."

" I'll get it done today, but I don't know how good a job it will be."

" Just do your best; that's all we ask."

" It's got no title, Sir. Do you want it run without one? "

Frank and the Judge looked at each other. " Just title it ' Defense of Fort McHenry,' " the Judge said. " Is that all right, Frank? "

Frank nodded. " I'll be back this afternoon," he said to the boy.

He went on to the Fort with the Judge, but he couldn't keep his mind off the poem and the boy George Sands. By midafternoon he was back at the printing office. He heard the thump of the press as he stepped in the door. He's running it, he thought. He's running my poem! There was a tremendous excitement in him.

The boy looked up. " Mr. Key! Come and see how you like it."

Frank stepped to his side. The black ink on the white sheet stared at him like something foreign. " Is that it? " he asked.

" Sure. That's it. Take one of the dry ones." The boy indicated a pile of narrow handbills, and Frank picked one up.

" O say, can you see, by the dawn's early light,
　　What so proudly we hailed at the twilight's last
　　　　gleaming,
　　Whose broad stripes and bright stars — — "

There was a lump in his throat as he read. He could hardly wait to get home to show it to Polly.

" The Judge will be in to get the rest of the copies," he said. " I'll just take along a few. I have to catch the coach for Frederick — "

" That'll be fine, Sir. How do you think it looks? "

" Fine! I don't see a mistake. You don't know how much we appreciate your running these."

" Oh, that's all right. Glad to oblige."

Frank took a dozen of the small handbills and went to wait for the coach.

It was a two-day journey to Frederick. As the coach jogged along through the autumn countryside, Frank found that he was very tired. He dozed much of the time, but was frequently awakened by an abrupt stop of the coach and the shouts of the coachman telling the good news of Fort McHenry.

At last they reached Frederick. He stopped briefly to see Ann and Roger Taney, borrowed a horse from their stables, and was on his way again.

It was past midnight when he turned his borrowed horse into the lane leading to the big brick house where he had been born. Almost at once lights began to twinkle in the windows — first one upstairs; then one down; another and another. Frank smiled. They had heard his horse's hoofs. Polly must have been sleeping very lightly!

By the time he reached the hitching rack, the dogs were barking and feet were running from the slave quarters. The front door burst open, and Frank thought of the times he had returned to Terra Rubra from school. But this time Polly stood between his mother and father, framed in the light from the door; and crowding around them to tumble down the steps were his three oldest children: Elizabeth, Maria, and Frank Junior. Polly had allowed them to get up.

The children reached him first. " Papa! Papa! Where have you been so long? What happened? "

" Are you all right, Frank? " Polly asked, her arms clinging to him.

" The rightest I've ever been! "

She caught the new note in his voice. " Frank, what is it? "

" I'll tell you a little later."

There was a welcoming fire in the big family sitting room. How dear and familiar everything looked! The worn, comfortable furniture; his mother's face, lovelier than ever, framed in gray hair; his father, still straight and tall; Polly and the children. " How are the little ones? " he asked.

" Fine," Polly said. " Upstairs sleeping like three little angels."

" Did Daniel's tooth come through? "

" It's through. Now tell us about you."

Frank stretched his long legs toward the fire. He was very tired, but he thought he had never been so happy.

" We brought the doctor back to Baltimore."

" You were successful! I knew you would be," Polly cried.

" And the war? " his father asked.

Frank smiled at him. " That's the best part," he said. " Fort McHenry sent the British fleet scampering."

Then he told them the whole story. The children were curled on the floor at his feet. Polly had drawn a hassock up at his knee. His mother and father sat on a love seat on the other side of the fire.

" And in the morning," he ended, and his voice choked, " when I saw the flag still flying, I wrote this — I *had* to write it! " He pulled the printed copies of his poem from his pocket and handed one to Polly.

" Read it aloud, Daughter," Mr. Key said as Polly took the folded sheet.

" O say, can you see — " Polly began. She read it through to the end, her voice pulsing with emotion. Then she turned her face up to Frank. " O darling! It's wonderful! " she said. Her voice was full of pride and deep joy.

Frank reached for her hand.

" The Star-spangled Banner," she said. " You changed the old line; this one is better." Suddenly she jumped up. " That's what you must call it! " she cried. " ' The Star-spangled Banner ' — instead of this awful title. O Frank, everyone will be singing it! "

" It's what the country needs," Mr. Key said, his voice husky, " a rousing song of patriotism."

" Let's sing it! " Frank Junior cried suddenly. " It says, ' To the tune of " To Anacreon in Heaven." ' How's it go, Papa? "

Frank looked embarrassed.

" He's right," Polly said. " Here, Frank Junior, pass a copy to your grandma and grandpa. We'll all sing it. You'll have to lead us, Frank."

So Frank began to sing, and the others joined in: " O say, can you see, by the dawn's early light — "

The dawn light was breaking as they finished.

The others went up the stairs to bed, but Frank and Polly lingered before the fire.

" Polly," Frank said, " at long last, I've done something that satisfies me. I am content."

" I knew it," Polly said softly. " Frank, I'm so glad. You've done something truly great for our nation. I feel it. It was what you had to do to fulfill the greatness within you."

ABOUT THE AUTHOR

M arion Marsh Brown is just an ordinary wife and mother, who works in her church, her P.T.A., and various community projects, even as the mothers of the young people who read her books. But because she likes to write — and likes teen-agers — she puts her " in-between time " into writing books.

She was born on a farm near Brownville, Nebraska, and went to school in the proverbial " little red schoolhouse." Because attendance was small, she was allowed to progress at her own rate of speed, so she found herself with an eighth grade diploma before her twelfth birthday.

Her high school work was done in Auburn, Nebraska. She graduated in three years, and the following fall started to college at the Nebraska State Teachers College at Peru, Nebraska. Here her interest in writing found new fuel. She wrote for the college newspaper and yearbook. Other interests too kept her busy. She gave her first piano recital. She went out for amateur theatricals. She was voted " Most Representative Girl on the Campus." And she found the two things she wanted to do with her life — teach and write. She graduated with an

A.B. degree at the age of eighteen, with highest honors and membership in the national English fraternity Sigma Tau Delta and the national education fraternity Kappa Delta Pi.

The next few years found her pursuing her two ambitions: teaching English in high schools in Nebraska and writing columns and feature articles for various newspapers and magazines.

In the meantime she had begun work on her Master's degree, which she received with a major in English from the University of Nebraska before she had reached her twenty-first birthday. It was during a summer's graduate work at the University of Minnesota that she met the man who was to become her husband, an Omaha attorney. After returning to the State Teachers College that was her Alma Mater, to be on the faculty in the Department of English for three years, she became Mrs. Gilbert S. Brown and took up her residence in Omaha.

Writing-wise, she was never idle. She reported news, did feature stories, wrote for radio, and did an occasional short story. In 1940 her son, Paul, was born, and as soon as he was old enough to listen she began making up stories for him. These afterward found their way into print. As her son outgrew the younger stories, she began writing for older children, and in the fall of 1949, her first book, *Young Nathan*, was released. It was a Junior Literary Guild selection. The following fall, her second book, *The Swamp Fox*, was published and won a Boys Clubs of America award. In the spring of 1953, her third book, *Frontier Beacon*, was published.